THE FAITH AND PRACTICE OF
THE QUAKERS

" The Quakers, of all Christian bodies, have remained nearest to the teaching and example of Christ."

DEAN W. R. INGE, in *The Platonic Tradition in English Religious Thought.*

THE
FAITH AND PRACTICE
OF THE QUAKERS

by
Rufus M. Jones

Friends United Press
Richmond, Indiana

ISBN 0-913408-57-3
Published by Friends United Press, Richmond, Indiana
Cover design: Susanna Combs

EDITOR'S PREFACE

A WORD of explanation seems to be needed in regard to the title and the sub-title which have been chosen for this series.

There is *one* faith, says St. Paul; but the title of the series indicates more than one. A difficulty unquestionably exists at that point. It has not been overlooked.

Had the promoters of this series adopted the former point of view and called it "the Faith" instead of "the Faiths," they would have answered in advance an important question which the series itself should be left to answer. But, equally, by calling the series "the Faiths," instead of "the Faith," have they not prejudged the question in another way?

Of the two positions the latter seemed the less dogmatic. Let us take the world as we find it, in which the Faiths show themselves as a plurality, and then, if they are really one, or many varieties of the same, or if only one is true and the rest false, let the fact appear from the accounts they give of themselves.

On no other terms could full liberty have been accorded to the writers who contribute to the series; on no other terms could the task of editing the series be fairly carried out. It would have been obviously unfair to demand of each of the contributors that he should exhibit the faith that is in him as ultimately identical with the faith that is in each of his fellow contributors. It would have been obviously unfair to deny to any contributor the right to exhibit his own faith as the only true faith and all the rest as false. It would have been obviously unfair to assume that faith is necessarily singular because St. Paul so describes it. For the degree of authority to be attributed to the words of St. Paul is precisely one of the points on which the contributors to the series must be allowed to differ and to speak for themselves.

The same considerations apply to the sub-title of the series—" Varieties of Christian Expression." It may be that Christianity has only *one* mode of expression, and that it ceases to be Christianity when expressed in any other way. But to take that for granted would ill become the editor of such a series as this, and it would become him still worse if he deliberately planned the series so as to lead up to that conclusion. Again we must take the world as we find it. Among those who claim to be Christians many varieties of expression unquestionably exist which may or may not be only different ways of expressing the same original truth. So far as the editor is concerned this must be left an open question. If to some writers in the series it should seem good to deny the name of Christian to those whose modes of expression differ from their own, they must not be precluded from doing so, and the reader will judge for himself between the claim and the counter-claim. Certainly the hope is entertained that from the presentation of differences in this series there may emerge some unities hitherto unsuspected or dimly seen ; but that will be as it may. The issue is not to be forced.

To present a complete logical justification of our title and sub-title is perhaps not possible, and such justification as we have here offered will probably commend itself only to the pragmatic mind. But objections taken to these titles will be found on examination to be objections to the series itself. How, we might ask, can any earnest and eminent Christian, believing his own variety of Christian expression to be better than the rest, logically justify his co-operation, in such a series as this, with other earnest and eminent Christians whose beliefs in that matter run counter to his own ? None the less they are here co-operating.

That such co-operation has been found possible may be reckoned one of the signs of the times. The explanation of it lies, not in logic, but in charity.

L. P. JACKS

CONTENTS

THE FAITH AND PRACTICE
OF THE QUAKERS

CHAPTER I

INTRODUCTION

THERE have been many transition periods in the
long history of the Christian Church, and this is
not the only such period that has seemed to the
thoughtful observers of the time to be critical for
religion. But there are many sound reasons for the
judgment that this is at least one of the most momentous
of all the transition epochs through which the Church
has ever passed. It can well be predicted, I think, that
when the Church emerges from this period of transition,
it will come forth more profoundly transformed than
was the case at the Reformation, or at any other epoch
since Pentecost. If that profound transformation here
predicted does not occur, it will be because something
much more serious than transformation has happened.
If the Church is too deeply intrenched in its ancient
system and dogma to adjust to the new situation which
confronts us and to the expansion of truth and light
now going on, then the Church will become a congealed
and rigid institution, out of contact with the onward
march of life and thought, left behind in the unfolding

1

process and useless as an organ of the Spirit—a withered branch. The hundred per cent. conservative may think that he is " saving " the Church by his resistance to progress, but he is " saving " it only by a method of shrinkage and arrested development, which looks very much like another form of " losing " it. Failure to adjust to the progress of expanding life is only another way of spelling death.

The issue now before us is not merely one between the scientific interpretation of the universe and the Biblical interpretation of it. If it were solely *that*, it could in time be settled by the gradual process of thought, for the mind can in the end answer the questions which the mind asks. If one answer is right and the other answer is wrong, some day the right position will conquer the wrong, and truth will drive error from the field.

The difficulty confronting us is deeper than that. Some of the foremost scholars of the age and some of the greatest living scientists of our time are in the Church, so that we are not confronted with an array of non-Christian scientists lined up against a Church composed of untrained and ignorant men who are defending superstitions. The disturbing thing is the present widespread *attitude of mind* in the world around us toward organized religion. There is a serious loss of interest in it. It is treated as negligible by a great many persons who, except for this attitude, are thoroughly good persons. It seems obvious, however, at the same time that there is no slackening of interest in vital religion, in a religion of life. When a book appears which presents in a fresh and living way the essential features of religious faith, or which interprets the personality of Jesus Christ in warm and appealing fashion, it immediately becomes the "best seller". The rank and file of people are keenly interested as soon as a famous writer, or a prominent person in any field, tells about his personal religion. It is always good "copy". Any fresh note on the old subject is hailed with enthusiasm. Any person who shakes himself free from conventions and breaks forth with a straightforward and sincere interpretation of practical religion gets all the hearing he wants. There is a good deal of evidence that religion is a *live* topic in our busy world of to-day and that it holds its place of high importance as a real issue of life to fully as great a degree as in any one of the last nineteen centuries. If it is true, as I believe it is, that religion as a fundamental trait of human life is still quick and vital, while there is at the same time a prevailing lack of interest in the organized Church, in its ministries, its offices and its services, there is good reason for supposing that the Churches of our time need to undergo a profound transformation, if they are to interpret God and if they are to minister to life in the world to-day.

When we seriously ask what is the matter with the Churches, we raise a question which cannot receive any easy, simple answer. We are confronted, as I have said, not alone by an intellectual issue, but by a more or less inarticulate *attitude of mind*. To use the famous phrase of George Fox, the Churches do not "speak to the condition" of the time. They are organized and equipped for a different generation than the one that happens just now to be here. It is something like an army with bows and arrows suddenly called upon to meet an army furnished with mauser rifles, machine guns and "big Berthas"; or like a teacher prepared for teaching multiplication and subtraction who is unexpectedly confronted with a class of students wanting to learn calculus, or fluxions. The debates which occur in most Church conferences and councils show how little the leaders comprehend the situation. They contend over matters which seem to the onlookers from without to be trivial and futile. It looks from an outside point of view like a Lilliputian battle over the question of whether eggs should be opened at the big end or the little end—a contest between " big-endians " and " little-endians ". Brought up, as so many theologians and churchmen are from their earliest days in a certain atmosphere and habit of thought, they find it well nigh impossible to stand off and to see the situation from the outside, or to get that first-hand feel of the utter inadequacy of these Church issues, which is so strong a feature in the lives of the great majority of people to-day.

In the first place, the Churches are bound to face, in a more adequate way than has yet been done, the intellectual reinterpretation of the universe. Christianity is, of course, vastly more than a theory of the universe. But at the same time, it cannot be right to hamper the freedom of the spiritual life of man by trying to keep it fitted into the intellectual framework of apostolic ages, or dark ages, or middle ages, or the reformation age. What one is asked to believe, or to think, or to hold, must fit in with and conform to one's whole system of thinking. Religious truth must always first of all be *truth*. It must not be *determined* by the views which prevailed in religious circles in some particular former century, any more than medical truth, or truth in physics, should be so determined. Every truth that has been discovered, verified and demonstrated, is thereby orthodox. Truth in this sphere and field, as in all other fields, grows, expands and enlarges. It must not be limited to what was in stock in the ages when creeds were formed. It is not enough, then, to debate a change of phrase here and there in an ancient formulation of faith. The person who is to be genuinely religious, who is to be a follower of Christ, must be free to believe what his deepest being finds to be true and he must not be asked to say that he believes what he cannot square with the facts of his universe, or with the testimony of his soul.

Every spiritual experience which those great Christian souls before our day have passed through, every word of prophetic insight which has come from them to us, is still precious and will assist us to find our way onward toward the fullness of truth and life, but the thoughtful person of this age feels that he should not be called upon to take over unchanged their world outlook or their intellectual findings. We need a type of Christianity that is brave enough to crown and mitre the individual in his search for truth and light, and which will use the conclusions and formulations of the past only as historical illustrations of the great spiritual adventure and as marked stages in the progress of the soul.

There is very widespread dissatisfaction with the type of preaching which for the most part prevails. It is built too much on antiquated models. It does not speak to the times. The sermon usually begins with a Scripture phrase or incident, and a large amount of time is often spent expounding the phrase or the incident. This may be done in a way that is valuable, but it is very apt to be lull and trivial. Where the dramatic issues of life stand out, or where great human traits come to light, or where the work of God through men of an earlier time is clear and vivid, then the exposition positively *counts*, but how often it is abstract or wooden ! Where, as in many instances, the preacher leaves exposition of Scripture and turns to deal with social or economic problems, the gain is slight. It often ceases to be preaching and becomes lecturing, and often enough it is lecturing by one who is ill-equipped for the field with which he is dealing. Men are not going to the churches in this busy world, crowded with calls and interests, to hear weak lectures. Nor are they going to Church to be entertained. As soon as a Church drops to the level of purveyor of entertainment, its doom is near and " mene " is written on it.

The Church, if it is to hold men, and keep its influence in the march of life, must be nothing less than a revealing place for God. It is *prophetic* ministry that serious people want—prophetic in the deepest sense. I mean by that a ministry that reveals God and interprets life in its nobler and diviner possibilities. People everywhere, especially young people, are confused in their thought of God. They have lost their sense of His reality. They discuss and seek and grope and doubt. They have little guidance and help. The old-fashioned answers and evidences do not convince. The problems are new ones. The questions come in different form. They cannot be answered by formula or by phrases. The young seekers want honest, sincere guides who understand the issues, who have travelled through the fog and the shadows and who have come out on the hill-top into the light.

A minister ought to be to all of us in our religious strivings what the artist is to those who are eager for beauty, or what the musician is to those who love music. The artist interprets beauty. He presents it in its convincing reality.

> Art was given for that;
> God uses us to help each other so,
> Lending our minds out.

And what is true of the artist's mission is no less true of the minister's. His business is making God real to men here—not entertaining them, or giving them a theory of society. It is no easy mission, that is clear enough, but it is the greatest one on earth, and there are many persons who have divine gifts for it. Let the Church become a revealing place and it will no longer need to apologize or advertise, its standing will be immediately settled.

I did not intend to speak slightingly of the social mission of the Church. The social mission is, and must always be, a great feature of real Christianity, only it must not take the place of the primary function, which is revealing God. There have been two marked tendencies in Christianity. On the one hand, the central concern has been to set forth a doctrine of salvation ; on the other, to build the kingdom of God. Salvation has usually been conceived in reference to the next world. It has been thought of in terms of a heaven of eternal joy, and it has quite naturally tended to become personal and egoistic. It has seemed to be such a momentous business that everything focused upon this achievement and all other things fell into the dim background. The Church with its hierarchy, its creeds and its sacraments, was thought of primarily as a mysterious instrument of salvation. In the light of that main business the importance of valid ordination, sound creed and efficacious sacraments dominated all other issues.

The other tendency is plainly paramount in Christ's primitive mission. One searches in vain for what He said about valid ordination, or sound creed, or efficacious sacraments, but the Gospels are full of interpretations of the kingdom of God which is to be built here. The term " kingdom of God " is a term of many meanings and there is disagreement among scholars about Christ's expectation of apocalpytic intervention. But one thing is sun-clear, namely, Christ's own way of life, to which He called His followers. His way of life at once points toward a new kind of world. It reverses competition and self-seeking. It trusts to the constructive power of love and grace and co-operation. Consecration to the life of others, self-giving, to the uttermost limits of sacrifice, are the very heart of it. The Cross is the sign in which He conquers and the way of the cross is the way of life and victory. The building of the new order of humanity, not by the propagation of a theory, but by the practice of the spirit of consecration and self-giving is, then, at least a possible meaning of the kingdom.

Whenever this second ideal has had sway in the faith and thoughts of men, great things have happened. Hospitals have been built, little children have received expert care and nurture the importance and preciousness of woman have been elevated, the freedom and enlargement of human life have become living concerns, and problems of health and healing have come strongly to the fore. There is most certainly a close connection between body and spirit, and Christianity has been at its best when this connection has been felt and appreciated. If we could realize once more, as Clement of

Alexandria did in the third century, that salvation is complete spiritual health, we should take a long step forward toward the building of a Church occupied with the tasks of remaking and transforming human life and human society.

Faith, Experience, and Service should be the great sacred words of our new Christianity. It is no doubt much more difficult to initiate a person into the Christian life on the basis of faith, experience and service than it is on the basis of a creed or a catechism. We pass over here from something fixed, definite and external— something to be learned by rote—to something more vague, shifting and inward. The task of training a Christian becomes more like that of training a person in art or music. The *soul* must now be trained as well as the memory. The individual must now work out his own salvation. He must win spiritual insight and not merely learn to recite something. He must face the fact that God is not a being to be read about in a book, but *a reality to be found and loved and worshipped.* He must discover that religion underlies all life and is not an appendix or addendum to it. Religion becomes the inspiration and spring that raises daily living to a new and wonderful stage of joy and power. On this basis, the organization would become something that the Church *is*, not something that it *has*, or has inherited and must maintain.

This brings us to a new difficulty that confronts the Church as it is to-day. Its organization is antiquated, as is its system of thought. It seems no doubt to many Christians that the antiquity of the structure of the Church is one of its greatest claims to reverence. Has it not come down unchanged from a divine and hoary past ? Does it not bear the marks of a divine origin and is not its *authority* due to just this glorious beginning ? Each one must answer such questions as that for himself, but the serious and thoughtful person of our time does not look for his evidence of divinity in origins. He looks for it in processes, in development, in achievement, in effectiveness. We do not find it easy to settle the origin of conscience. We estimate its worth and claim by its moral illumination and power, not by its primitive origin—by what it does, not by where it came from.

There is very little to indicate that Christ was concerned with founding an institution. His interest in the kingdom of God, and in a way of life, completely overtops His interest in the construction of a Church. The first stages of the life of the Church are dim and uncertain. There was a fellowship at first, rather than an authoritative organization. There was group life and power of growth, rather than system and structure. All through the formative period, what we call the apostolic period, the leaders are feeling their way. They have no map or plan. They meet emergencies and work through them in the wisest way possible. They give no hint or intimation that their solution is the only possible one. They do not claim that the road forward is on a divine chart which they have in their hands. Early churches had more than one form of organization, just as early interpreters of Christian truth gave more than one form of interpretation. There was large freedom and leeway and scope. They were all searching for the best and most effective way to transmit the precious truth and life committed to them.

In the long period of historical development, too, there has been steady adjustment to the demands of the situation. The Church has always been in the making. The finished model, or pattern, is laid up in no secret place, in mount or in sanctuary. Each temporary builder has done the best he could to follow his highest light and leading, but none of them has had infallible and indubitable directions or instructions. The Church has grown as other spiritual realities grow with the ages. There have been multitudinous tributaries flowing into the main central stream that has run on through the centuries. Some of the tributaries have manifestly altered the stream, but it is nevertheless a river of life, still effective for the healing of the nations.

There are two well-known ways of dealing with the spiritual contribution of the past, both of which ways are inadequate. There is (1) the way of the *authoritarian*. He assumes that the past settles what is to be accepted, received and venerated. There is, he believes, a matchless authority in the structure which has been built by the holy hands of the fathers. We turn to it as to a sacred ark of heavenly origin. It is not to be changed, it is to be preserved in its purity and transmitted to the future. Every feature of it is essential to its structure. Nothing must be added or subtracted. Every jot and tittle must be kept. We should lose the possibility of salvation if we lost " the efficacy and validity " that have come from the divine founders and transmitters. The criterion of spiritual truth and certainty is not in our own souls ; it is in the immemorial authority of the institution.

On the other hand, there is a strong alternative view. It is (2) the view of the *rationalist*. He makes little of the authority of the past. The past has no more authority than the present. Antiquity supplies no title-deeds to truth. Everything must run the gauntlet of scientific enlightenment. We must have verifiable facts. We must build only on what we know and can prove. The rationalist plays havoc with sacred writings and with venerable institutions. He insists on their writ of *quo warranto*. He analyses and dissects the most revered inheritances. He abhors superstition and he has a deep antipathy for dogmatism and underground assertion. He is in irreconciliable opposition to the authoritarian.

It seems hardly likely that the Church of the future —the spiritual Church which we are seeking—will be either the Church of the authoritarian or of the rationalist. Each of them represents a half-truth, each looks out on life with a large blind spot. The Church of the future will certainly not be of this old-fashioned authoritarian type. Its authority will be inward rather than outward. It will be due to a *present* quality of life and power and not to something in a remote past. But the new Christianity will not be clipped and pared down to the *cold residuum* of the rationalist. It will not fly in the face of facts. It will not defy rationality, as Tertullian did. It will respect history and science and the splendour of the mind. But it will insist on the recognition of the whole life and not merely on the rights of the intellect. A man's emotions and sentiments are as deep and significant as is his power of reasoning. We are what we are as much because we *feel* as because we *think*, and when we clap down the lid on our feelings we have wrecked our capabilities as men. We not only argue and prove, but we build ideals, we overpass what we see and touch. We live in the unseen and forecast what ought to be. We want a religion that *knows*, but we also want one that *loves and believes and appreciates*. Our new Church which is to speak to the condition of the time must have an authority, but that authority must be the authority of spiritual life and transforming power. It must have wisdom and insight, but it should be the wisdom and insight of experience rather than of formal logic and of reasoning.

This little book is written to present an historical experiment along these lines. It is three hundred years since George Fox was born, and the spiritual movement which he inaugurated has been tested now by two hundred and seventy-five years. The Quaker Society is still a small body and it presents a seemingly feeble front for the age-long battle of Armageddon. It is a tiny band of labourers for the task of building a spiritual civilization. But this is a matter in which *numbers* are not the main thing. The vital question, after all, is whether this small religious Society here in the world to-day is a living organ of the Spirit or not. Is it possessed by a *live* idea ? Is it in the way of life ? Has it found a forward path toward the new world that is to be built ? Is it an expansive, or a waning, power ? It has stood scorn and brutality; it has weathered the beatings and buffetings of a hostile world; it has survived its own blunders and stupid divisions. When now the world has become kind and friendly toward it, and is even eager for it to *prove* its divine mission, can it make a significant contribution to the truth and life and power of the Christianity that is to save and redeem the world ? Those questions can hardly be answered in this first edition. They must wait for the verdict of later history.

I shall endeavour in a very simple way to interpret the achievements, the aims and the ideals of the Quaker movement. No one knows its weaknesses and limitation more clearly than I do. I have no illusions. I have looked its history full in the face. I am acquainted with all the symptoms of its present ailments. But I am not writing now in order to tell that part of the story. I am concerned here to show what the Quaker movement has taken as its line of life and what it still hopes and believes its mission to be.

There will always be diversities in the Christian Church. It will never be possible to attain complete uniformity in thought or in forms of worship or in ways of interpreting religious history, nor is that desirable. There are characteristic varieties of mental type. Our outlooks are different. Our needs are different. Our range of thought and experience is different. We should as individuals belong, if possible, to a religious group, a spiritual family, that best fits our needs and aptitudes. We should not all be fused and merged into one uniform mould in one vast structure. We should have our denominational homes and we should worship where we find ourselves in most sympathetic accord with others. But our narrow *isms* should vanish. Our sectarian spirit should die out. Our rivalries and jealousies should cease. And we should all contribute to the one growing, expanding Church of the Spirit, which is being builded through the ages " for a habitation of God ".

The Quaker Society is one of these spiritual families with definite characteristics. It offers a denominational home of a specific type. It fits, and is congruous with, a well-known and well-defined mental outlook and habit of thought. It emphasizes certain very important aspects of religion. It cultivates a type of worship which seems to many vital and spiritual. It maintains a spirit and method of human service, which are greatly needed in the world to-day. It exhibits a warm and intimate type of inward religion. It is broad, inclusive and tolerant. It cares intensely for religious experience and discounts those aspects of religion which are argumentative, speculative and divisive. It has preserved a good degree of evangelical fervour, without becoming seriously entangled in the network of theology that often goes with the doctrinal word "evangelical". It has kept pretty close to the central meaning of the Incarnation, the definite breaking in of God into the course of history, the coming of eternity into the midst of time, in the form of a living, visible human-divine Person, through whom all life on its highest levels is to be interpreted. But it discovers no temporal *end* to that Life here in the world. The Christ who was a visible presence in Galilee and Judea is just as certainly alive and present now.

> The healing of His seamless dress
> Is by our beds of pain ;
> We touch Him in life's throng and press,
> And we are whole again.

The Friends are essentially Johannine in their religious faith and outlook. Their great religious words are found in the Fourth Gospel. They are, *light, truth, life, love, spirit, way*. They take the message at Jacob's well as the heart of their faith : " God is Spirit and they that worship Him must worship Him in spirit and in truth." They find their loftiest hopes expressed in the words : " I am the resurrection and the life ; he that believeth on me, though he die, yet shall he live ; and whosoever liveth and believeth on me shall never die." They look out on the future with their expectation grounded on the saying : " When He the

Spirit of truth is come, He shall guide you into all truth." Many of my readers, who will perhaps approve of these affirmative and vital features, will at the same time very likely miss something in this type of Christianity. They will feel that it is partial and one-sided. It will perhaps not appear to them to be complete and universal, wide and catholic enough to be a faith for the whole race. I shall not attempt to meet that criticism. The facts must be as they are. If there are other essential aspects of religion which the Quakers leave out of account, they must be looked for in other denominational families where they are stressed. Those who compose the Quaker family do not feel the need of them. They are satisfied with a few simple and vital realities. The following chapters will tell what those vital aspects are. Those who desire a fuller and more detailed interpretation of Quakerism should turn to the *Quaker History Series*, which I have edited, two golden volumes of which are by the late William Charles Braithwaite, to whose precious memory I dedicate this volume.

CHAPTER II

BRIEF HISTORY OF THE RISE OF FRIENDS AND THEIR SPIRITUAL BACKGROUND

TIME is a one-way street. The direction is continuously forward. Space admits of both directions—out and back—and many more ways of movement. Time, on the other hand, goes unvaryingly onward. A conscious spectator can *reflect* about the past and can roughly *recover* it in terms of memory, but in vain does he strive to travel backwards and *be* in a bygone moment. He is on an escalator which under no circumstances will reverse or alter its speed. We stand on a slender ridge of observation and look both ways, while the drama all the time moves steadily on. "No mortal ever dreams", Lowell wrote in his *Cathedral,*

> That the scant isthmus he encamps upon
> Between two oceans, one, the Stormy, passed,
> And one, the Peaceful, yet to venture on,
> Hath been that future whereto prophets yearned
> For the fulfilment of Earth's cheated hope,
> Shall be that past which nerveless poets moan
> As the lost opportunity of song.

The type of Christianity which I am to write about here—the Quaker Faith and Way of Life—is "a going concern". We catch it for the instant on our "narrow isthmus" of the present, but we cannot talk about it

C   17

or reveal its significance without looking backward and looking forward. It has come out of the tragedies and triumphs of long centuries of spiritual travail. It bears the scars and the tokens of the years of spiritual battle behind it. It is, too, what it is now partly because of what it proposes to be in the future. Forecasts determine the quality of the present almost as much as memories do. We can, however, deal with the forecasts better in later chapters. This will be the proper place to review the historical situation out of which the Society of Friends came to birth.

The Reformation was preceded by a long succession of attempts to transform or reform the Church. These attempts were very varied in type and in aim. In a rough and general way, they can be gathered up under two prevailing tendencies. Many of the reforming efforts were aimed against the manifest corruptions of the Church which were almost universally recognized. Many persons were disturbed over its obvious secularization. Many disapproved of mass, of purgatory, of prayers to saints, of indulgences and of pilgrimages. Many questioned the fundamental theory and the efficacy of the sacraments. These ideas and attitudes lay behind one large general type of anti-church movements. This stream was always fed by underground springs from those numerous dualistic sects of Europe which had sprung from the Manichæans, the Paulicians, the Bogomiles and the Cathari, all of them carrying a strand of Eastern influence. This connection with the dualistic sects is most obvious in the case of the Waldenses and the Albigenses, but it is likewise a factor in the Beghards, the Brethren of the Free Spirit, the Spiritual Franciscans, in Wyclif, and, of course, later in the Anabaptist movement.

The other tendency was not strongly anti-church like those above mentioned. It was rather a deep longing for greater spiritual reality, for a discovery of God and a more vital contact with Him, for a religion of life and experience in place of an elaborate ecclesiastical structure. There were many earnest, serious souls who were not " fed ". They were mystically minded and yearned for more guidance than they got in the cultivation of the interior life. They flocked with enthusiasm to hear Eckhart and Tauler preach, and similar eager spirits existed in almost all sections of Europe where there were not Taulers or Eckharts to hear. These quiet people in the land dwelt fondly on their glowing imaginative pictures of the apostolic Church, and they wanted above everything else to see a return to the golden age of faith and life in the Spirit. From the opening of the thirteenth century onward there was an unbroken stream of mystical religion. The great literary figures who most adequately voiced the movement were powerfully influenced by Neo-Platonic mysticism, as it had come into mediæval thought through St. Augustine on the one hand and Pseudo-Dionysius on the other ; but the rank and file who made up the mystical groups were simple folk who wanted to find God and to walk in the Spirit and who were bitterly disappointed over the secularized Church and disillusioned as to its spiritual mission.

These two wide-spread tendencies—the anti-church movements and the stream of mystical devotion—had a marked influence in effecting the Reformation, and both tendencies reappeared in emphatic forms in the years of stress and strain that followed Luther's dynamic strokes against the ancient system. The Anabaptists were influenced by the previous anti-church movements, and they shared, too, though in slight degree, in the mystical aspirations of the period. But one of the greatest forces which operated to produce the Anabaptist groups was Luther's powerful note of saving faith and the call to Christian freedom in his early proclamations. These ideas joined with the social, economic and political hopes surging in the hearts of the common people, gave the Anabaptist leaders their marching power. They were, too, brought under the spell of the New Testament which came to them like a fresh revelation from God, and they saw with kindled minds the new way of life and the new type of Church which these recently translated pages put before them. Most people do not even yet realize the full significance and the world-wide sweep of this root and branch reformation which attracted and fascinated the common man.

Much more restrained and more completely guided by well-trained scholars was another reforming movement which had pretty much the same ancestry as the Anabaptists. This was a somewhat sporadic and unorganized attempt at a radical transformation of the Church in the direction of mystical experience, a religion of the Spirit with a large degree of freedom from the doctrinal and ecclesiastical structure of the past. Those who became the leaders of this effort to bring about a radical transformation of the Church were at first loosely attached to the Anabaptist movement, but they gradually disassociated themselves from it and struck out a path of their own. They disapproved of stiff and rigid external organization. They were not interested in maintaining any fixed forms or sacraments. They discarded time-honoured theological systems and refused to be drawn into debates and discussions over abstract doctrines. Nearly all the men who held and expounded these ideas had been directly or indirectly influenced by Erasmus. They had strong humanist sympathies and took a broad and liberal attitude on most questions of human interest. They broke utterly with the Augustinian theory of depravity and original sin, and they sided with Pelagius in the view that every person is created and brought into the world with capacity of free choice for the good as well as for the evil. The dice, they held, are not loaded either way, though the customs and habits of the centuries have no doubt done much to spoil the Eden of innocence into which the little child is born. They maintained, on the other hand, that every new-comer to the world is endowed with a spark of divine light within the soul, and is drawn forward toward goodness by inward cords of grace. They believed that the external, or visible, Church, as they called it, had always been too corrupt, worldly and political-minded to be an organ of the Spirit, and they felt sure that the reformed Church, with its external systems and its alliance with the State, would go the same way. They stood, therefore, for an invisible Church rather than a visible one. They wanted to spread truth and love by spiritual methods rather than by ecclesiastical methods—by the influence of personality, by inspiration, by leadership, by contagion rather than by organization.

They have been called, and, in fact, they sometimes called themselves, " spiritual reformers ". They were mystics, though they discarded the elaborate mystical and metaphysical systems inherited from St. Augustine and Pseudo-Dionysius. They were as simple and direct in their interpretation of mystical experience as they were in their ideas about the Church. Each person should find his contacts with God and should work out his relations with his divine Companion as best suited his needs and his disposition, without regard to any clamping systems of past ages. The best known exponents of this loosely-knit way of life and faith are Hans Denck and Sebastian Franck of Germany, Sebastian Castellio of France, later of Switzerland, Camillo of Sicily, Dirck Coornhert of Holland, and later a little group of English leaders of whom I shall speak. On the Continent, the movement culminated in the formation of a body of Christians known as " Collegiants ", or " Seekers ". They had only the loosest organization, no ordained clergy, no sacraments, no creeds, no ritual. They met on Sundays for divine worship, sitting for the most part in silence, but having an occasional prayer or public " message ", as some one felt " moved " to speak. They regarded this plan of theirs, however, as only an " interim " arrangement, while they were " waiting " and " seeking " for a fresh revelation from God of the nature of " the true Church ", which He would, they believed, set up in His own time and in His own way by a new apostolic anointing.

All these and many other reforming and transforming movements found voice in one way or another in England. Anabaptist groups appeared there almost as soon as they did on the Continent, and in the face of severe persecution they persisted and were never wholly suppressed. The ideas of the spiritual reformers travelled across the Channel and took root. John Everard, D.D. (1575–1650), was the first prominent purveyor and interpreter, known to us, of these ideas. Everard translated and printed extracts from the writings of Denck, Franck, Castellio and earlier mystics, and as Rector of St. Martin-in-the-Fields he preached many sermons now preserved in *Some Gospel Treasures Opened*, which set forth the same inward religion and the same call for an invisible and spiritual Church. Giles Randall, of Chipping Wycombe, an Oxford scholar (B.A. at Lincoln College in 1626), translated a number of the little spiritual books which contained the essential message of this spiritual movement. Francis Rous (1579–1659), Peter Sterry (died 1672), John Saltmarsh (died 1647) and William Dell (died 1664) are some of the most impressive English exponents of this type of faith and life. Jacob Boehme, of Görlitz, in Silesia (1575–1624), an untutored philosopher and mystic, worked out an extensive and complicated system of alchemy, theosophy and mysticism, which was deeply penetrated with the spiritual outlook and the inward type of salvation which the spiritual reformers taught. All Boehme's books were translated into English between the years 1647 and 1661, and there were enthusiastic Boehme disciples in many parts of England.

Besides these groups and influences, there were many small sects in England which cultivated a mystical and non-ecclesiastical type of piety. One of the most interesting of these sects was the Family of Love, which owed its origin to a Westphalian mystic named Henry Nicholas, who was born about 1501. This Family of Love was a Fellowship of persons who lived a quiet, simple, community life. They disapproved of professional ministers and of the historic Church, and they endeavoured to live Christlike lives and to practise a spirit of love and brotherhood. There were, too, especially in Yorkshire, Cumberland and Westmorland, large groups of Seekers, very similar to the Collegiants of Holland. During the unsettled years of the Civil War and the Commonwealth, there were thus multitudes of persons who were detached from the Anglican communion, who at the same time felt a marked disapproval of Calvinistic forms of thought and organization, and who were struggling to create what they thought of as an apostolic type of Christianity, something like that which the spiritual reformers had longed for. Out of these movements and out of this spiritual atmosphere Quakerism emerged.

Many of the first members of the Society of Friends arrived at their peculiar religious views and their way of life before they met George Fox, so that it is evident that the fundamental ideas of the movement were more or less " in the air " in the Commonwealth period. But, at the same time, he is the dynamic figure of the new group and he deserves to be called the founder of the Society. One is fortunate to live at a time when great forces are at work, quickening the minds of men with eager expectation that all things are about to be made new. The twenty years from 1640 to 1660 in England was such an epoch. No one knew what was to happen, but it was a time of general tip-toe expectation. " One never goes so far ", Oliver Cromwell once said, " as when he doesn't know where he is going ! " That was the feature of this period. There was the sound of " a going in the mulberry-trees ", a vague, mysterious heaving of hope in all hearts, an onward yearning of unstilled desire, but no one knew quite what was wanted or where the true promised land lay. Fox became a leader toward Canaan without ever having dreamed that he was designed to be a leader.

His origin was humble, though the stock of which he came was of excellent quality on both his father's and mother's side of the house. There were rugged, solid traits of character in the father, Christopher, with good sense and moral fibre, and the mother, Mary Lago, came of martyr stock and possessed a quiet, tender, deeply religious spirit. Their son, George, was born in Fenny Drayton in July 1624, and showed from early childhood an unusual religious bent, while at the same time he was shy, retiring, and meditative. He had almost no systematic education, growing up as a peasant labourer, tending sheep and cattle in the fields and working on occasion as a shoe-maker. He was, however, well endowed with mental gifts and capacity, and he was keen and alert on all questions of spiritual import. He became a diligent reader of the English Bible and he seems early in years to have been sorely distressed by the stern Calvinist theology which he heard from the Reverend Nathaniel Stephens in the Fenny Drayton church. There appeared to him to be a sharp conflict between the simple religion of the Gospels and this monumental system of theology, and a no less marked discrepancy between the apostolic way of life and the method of life which characterized the formal Church members whom he knew. This situation threw the sensitive youth into serious mental conflict, upset his peace and finally led him to the verge of despair. He left home, broke his Church relationship and went out alone into the world to seek for spiritual counsel and guidance. He could find no wise guides or helpers, and he came to the conclusion that the Church was lost in the wilderness and that ministers were empty talkers without spiritual experience, inspiration, power or divine authority.

One can guess, though there is little in the *Journal* to establish the point, that in his travels and his quests he was brought into contact with persons who held the looser, freer ideas of the spiritual reformers, the Seekers, the Anabaptists, the Family of Love and other fermenting sectaries. He could hardly travel as he did on a religious search for light in the England of this period without making such contacts. He would find in many communities little books and tracts which were regarded by ecclesiastical authorities to be " dangerous ", but which would give him suggestions and flashes of illumination. He would talk with those who were as dissatisfied and as disillusioned as he was over the external forms of Christianity. Brooding, meditating, reading his Bible, feeling the ferment and aspirations of the common people, his soul slowly began to find its direction. Insights, " openings ", as he calls them, broke in on his thoughts. They were, plainly enough, in line with the hopes and longings of the scattered spiritual sectaries, but they came to him now with a freshness and a first-hand conviction which made them seem to him to be his own discoveries of new truth. He had rare mystical moments when the light of God burst into his soul and he felt as though he had the key to all the store-houses of divine grace. The whole creation took on " a new smell ", as though the lily of the new dispensation had suddenly bloomed. He saw that there is an ocean of darkness and death in the world, but an infinite ocean of light and love flowed over the ocean of darkness, and he felt himself called to be an apostle of this light and love.

We have in Fox a man who felt himself called to be a religious reformer. He was a mystic, not a scholastic or a rationalist. He was a prophet, not a priest or a scribe. He knew extremely little Church history ; he had as good as no theological learning ; he was not even well versed in the literature of the movements which prepared the way for his mission. He well nigh knew the Bible by heart, but he had no historical knowledge of its background and no critical insight into the original meaning of texts or the purpose and significance of the different books of the great volume which he loved. He depended on flashes and openings and he turned most naturally to the luminous passages which proclaimed inward religion and announced the light and guidance of the Spirit. Under the constructive and integrating power of his experiences and his convictions, he became a strong and vigorous personality. He was changed from a weak, shy and timorous youth to a robust and fearless man. When once he had unsealed his commission and felt assured of his call, there was nothing on earth that could daunt him or terrify him. His greatest danger was not from without; it was from within. He broke with external authority; he had at the first few good counsellors; he was subject to visions; he was swept with enthusiasms; he was living in a time of seething dreams and expectations; he was visited by ranters and fanatics, yet he kept his head and, with slight exceptions, maintained his balance. Each year saw him growing steadier and wiser, and he came through the turmoils and the testings with sanity, poise and judgment. William Penn very finely says of him: " I write my knowledge and not report, and my witness is true, having been with him for weeks and months together on diverse occasions, and those of the nearest and most exercising nature, and that by night and by day, by sea and by land, in this and in foreign countries, and I can say I never saw him out· of his place, or not a match for every service or occasion."

When Fox started forth, in 1647–8, to be, as he believed, the prophet and apostle of a new and completer reformation, his battle-idea was the continuous revelation of God's will in the soul of man. He had been convinced by his own experience, by the testimony of those whom he met among the spiritual sects, and finally by great texts in Scripture, that there is a direct illumination from God within man's inner being. He met the Calvinistic theory of a congenital seed of sin in the new-born child by the counter claim that *there is a seed of God in every soul*. This " seed " or " light ", which he proclaimed, was thought of as a *capacity of response* to divine intimations and openings, a basis of inward communication and correspondence between God and man and a moral searchlight revealing to man the absolute distinction between right and wrong, making the path of righteousness and truth unmistakable. When he began his itinerant ministry, he had not thought through the implications of his discovery ; he had, of course, made no psychological or philosophical analysis of the ground for such a faith—he had merely leaped to the height of his great conviction, and he felt at once that it put Christianity on a new basis of authority. The master key was in the hand of the individual man. Nobody else could " open and shut ". The significant and eternal realities are those inward decisions, when the soul says " yes " or " no " to God. Fox no doubt overstressed the range and scope of inward guidance. He made it more specific, concrete and detailed than most of us find it to be. He thought that the organ of revelation in us was like a new sense that opened up a whole new world of life, and the scenery and circumstance of it, in minute detail, could infallibly come through to us. He made communication easier and more common than the facts will warrant, but at all events, the momentous truth seemed clear to him that religion rests in the last resort not on a book or on a church but on the fundamental nature of man's inner being. To his positive religious message, Fox joined a searching criticism of the organized Church and of many of the social customs of the time. He was strongly opposed to " priests ", attacking them in the main on two counts : (1) That they were " hirelings ", and (2) that they interpreted Christianity merely as theory, instead of being men who were shining examples on account of their experience of God and of their practice of Christ's way of life. He was not always fair in his judgment on these matters, but it must be said that there was much on the second count to support his general attitude toward the ministers whom he met. His attack on " steeple-houses " was due, partly, at least, to the fact that the church spire and the cathedral stood in his mind as relics and symbols of the unreformed Church, and they aroused in him a sweep of emotional, rather than a rational, hostility. His opposition to music and art was for the most part not very sound. He saw the easy misuse of music ; he was disturbed by ribald songs and plays, and he felt that it was all too easy in religious services to sing words the meaning of which the singer had not experienced or did not understand. But he was, nevertheless, hurried with too little ground for it into an attitude of sweeping opposition to these two great forms of culture and these important sources of happiness. His contemporary, Richard Baxter, staunchly Puritan in his attitude toward life and yet usually very broad in his sympathies, expressed his feelings about music in these quaint words : " For myself, I confess that harmony and melody are the pleasure and elevation of my soul and have made a Psalm of Praise in the Holy Assembly the chief delightful exercise of my religion and my life ; and hath helped to bear down all the objections which I have heard against Church music. . . . Let those that savour not melody, leave others to their different appetites and be content to be so far strangers to their delights."

It is odd that one who was so completely opposed to Puritan theology and ecclesiastical authority as George Fox was should nevertheless have out-puritaned the Puritans in his desire to free life from its complexities and frivolities. There is often a modicum of principle and good sense behind his attempts to curtail and simplify social etiquette, but he pushed his scruples against the removal of the hat, against the use of " you " to a single person, and against the names of the days and months to an absurd importance. Deep-lying springs of emotion were at work in him in these matters and the rational element was slight. At a later period in the history of Quakerism, all these minor testimonies were felt to be on a different ground from the one which really explains their origin.

Fox met from the very first an onslaught of abuse and persecution. In the early stage, it was to a large extent the free play of wild sport and mob violence. He met this display of brute hostility with remarkable courage and in splendid spirit, often conquering it by his humour, by his mother wit, or by his spirit of Christian nobility. His arrests and imprisonments were on various grounds. On at least one occasion he interrupted a minister with whom he disagreed. Sometimes he was charged with blasphemy under the loose blasphemy laws of the period. Sometimes he was suspected as a political plotter. Sometimes he refused to take an oath of loyalty because of his opposition to any kind of an oath whatever. Sometimes he came into collision with the laws which enjoined or safe-guarded " uniformity ". On all counts he was brought before courts and magistrates sixty times, and he was imprisoned eight times for longer or shorter terms, covering in all about six years.

At first, Fox propagated his ideas alone and unaided, but he found in his travels persons of kindred views and spirit, and he soon had an occasional helper and fellow-traveller. In this early period, Elizabeth Hooton, James Nayler and William Dewsbury were his most important helpers. In 1652 he found communities of Seekers in the northern counties who were " con-vinced " in large numbers and joined his movement enthusiastically. They not only swelled the number of his adherents, but, what was more important, they furnished him with a strong band of well-trained exponents of his type of spiritual Christianity who were at the same time loyal to his leadership. Some of the strongest leaders of martyr fibre who came out of this " convincement " were Francis Howgill, Edward Bur-rough, John Audland, Richard Hubberthorne, John Camm and Thomas Taylor. They knew exactly where kindred bodies of believers in England were to be found and they often knew, too, of prominent sympathizers whom Fox by himself could hardly have discovered. The result was that the band of " Children of the Light ", as they first called themselves, grew by leaps and bounds. From now on, the movement had vigorous preachers and effective pamphleteers, and in spite of mobs and prisons it made converts by the thousands, the adherents being usually drawn from groups of people who were in revolt from the churches and who were already prepared for the experiment of the light within. From 1652 Swarthmoor Hall, in the Lake District, became the central rallying place of the expanding movement. Margaret Fell, its mistress, became one of the most important and influential members of the Quaker group, and her distinguished husband, Judge Thomas Fell, though never actually joining the Society, gave generous and substantial support to it.

At a later period of George Fox's life, there was a second group of important "convincements", the most influential in its effect upon the expansion of Quakerism in the Colonies being that of William Penn, who was "convinced" in 1667. He became one of the foremost champions and defenders of religious liberty in England, the founder of one of the greatest American colonies, as a "holy experiment", and the author of notable essays and treatises written often in a style of rare charm and beauty. Robert Barclay, a Scotchman of distinguished family and of refined and extensive learning, was "convinced" in 1666, and became the greatest early interpreter of the Quaker conception, publishing the first edition of his *Apology for the True Christian Divinity, as the same is held forth and preached by the people, Called, in scorn, Quakers* in 1678. It was an epoch-making book both for the challenge it made to Christian scholars everywhere and even more for the effect it produced during the next two centuries upon the Friends themselves. Isaac Penington was "convinced" somewhat earlier than Penn and Barclay. He and his wife, Mary, had passed through a long and serious period of preparation for the message of the Light. They had already broken with the Church, held views of the spiritual reformer type and were, in a loose sense of the word, " Seekers " About the year 1658, Isaac Penington attended a Quaker meeting for worship which powerfully moved him. As the knowledge of the truth broke into his conscience, he said in his heart : " This is He, this is He, there is no other ; This is He whom I have waited for and sought after from my childhood, who was always near me and had begotten life in my heart, but I knew Him not distinctly, or how to receive Him or dwell with Him. . . . I have met with my God ; I have met with my Saviour. . . . I have felt the healings drop upon my soul from under His wings ". He was one of the most mystically minded of all the early Friends, and, being possessed of literary gifts, he expressed impressively their deep mystical aspirations and experiences. At about the same time, 1659, Thomas Ellwood was " convinced " at a meeting in Buckinghamshire. He says of the effect of it : " I drank in the words with desire, for they not only answered my understanding but warmed my heart with a certain heat, which I had not till then felt from the ministry of any man ". Thomas Ellwood was a good scholar. A little later he became secretary to John Milton and suggested to the poet the writing of *Paradise Regained*. His most important contribution to Quakerism was his work as editor of the famous *Journal of George Fox*, produced from Fox's personal Narratives, Travel Diaries, Notes, Letters and Documents. It was first published in 1694.

The first Quakers landed in Boston in July 1656, coming thither from Barbadoes. They were two women, Mary Fisher and Ann Austin. They were

D

transported to Barbadoes after being kept five weeks in solitary confinement. Two days after they were transported, nine more Quaker missionaries sailed into Boston harbour. They were imprisoned eleven weeks without being allowed to " contaminate " anybody and then were transported. The first successful " invasion " of the colony was made by eleven Quakers, six of whom had been in the earlier party of eight, in 1657, in the ship *Woodhouse*, which was owned by a Quaker, Robert Fowler, who navigated it himself. They stopped on the way to plant their seed on Long Island and then landed at Newport, Rhode Island, and dispersed from there through Massachusetts. They met with extraordinary success, for, as had been the case in England, they found " Seekers " in many places, notably in Sandwich, Lynn and Salem, and, of course, everywhere in Rhode Island. The " Seed ", as the Quakers loved to call their faith, spread rapidly, and aroused the Puritan authorities to a fierce attempt at suppression, which resulted in four martyrdoms and a tragic amount of sufferings under " bloody laws ". But in the end the Quakers outwearied their persecutors and won their place in the great Bay Colony. They spread rapidly in Long Island and other parts of the Dutch Colonies. They grew strong in Maryland, Virginia and the Carolinas. George Fox visited the American Colonies in 1671–3, and a great expansion of Quakerism followed from his travels and ministry. In 1674 two Quakers bought the proprietary rights to the western half of New Jersey, and in 1681 William Penn and eleven others, probably all Friends, bought the eastern half of New Jersey. That same year, 1681, Charles II conveyed by charter to William Penn as Proprietor the land now known as Pennsylvania.

William Penn came in person in 1682 to found Philadelphia and to launch his Holy Experiment in Government. There were between 50,000 and 60,000 Friends in England when George Fox died, in 1691, and there cannot have been much fewer than that number in America in 1700.

The original name of the Friends, as I have said, was " the Children of the Light ". But as early as 1652 they began to call themselves " Friends ", sometimes the phrase " Friends in the Truth " was used. They were influenced in their use of the name by Christ's words : " I have called you friends ", and they used the word to express both a fact and an ideal—they were to be a people who should literally be " friends ". The term " Society of Friends " does not occur before 1665 and did not come into general use until the second period of Fox's ministry—the organizing period. The word " Quaker " was first used by Justice Gervase Bennett, of Derby, in 1650 as a term of reproach. The word had been used earlier for *trembling sectaries*, and there is plenty of evidence that Friends did literally tremble or quake with emotion in their meetings, so that Justice Bennett's term had some fitness, as Fox himself more than once allowed. It has now come to be a name in quite general usage both outside and inside the Society of Friends and no longer carries any stigma.

This sketch presents in the briefest possible way how there ever came to be a Quaker branch of the Christian faith. I shall next proceed to set forth the main features of this type of Christianity.

CHAPTER III

THE TYPE OF CHRISTIANITY

GEORGE FOX and his contemporary Friends sincerely believed that they were engaged in the momentous business of reproducing in the world the New Testament type of Christianity. One of their most common phrases was, " primitive Christianity revived ", and that stood in their minds as an exact equivalent for what the world called " Quakerism ". They did not favour any word ending in " ism ". They never remotely thought of themselves as forming, or belonging to, a " sect ", or a " denomination ". They were engaged, as they believed, in reviving Christianity in its original form and power, and they believed implicitly that their " truth ", as they called it, would eventually sweep the world, convince, and finally include all branches of Christendom. They were not starting something new and divisive, but were rather recovering something that had been lost, like the prodigal, and found again. The Church, they assumed, had lost its vision and power soon after the death of the first apostles. It dropped, according to their view, to a new low level in the time of Constantine, and from then on it ceased to be an organ of the Spirit. The Reformation, both in England and on the Continent, they felt, only " reformed " the old Church and failed to restore the original spirit, power and authority of the apostolic Church.

They believed that at last all things were being made new. Fox seemed to them a new apostle, a divinely chosen messenger of the Spirit to inaugurate a spiritual era. They believed that he was commissioned with divine authority to end the time of apostasy and wilderness wandering, and to begin the new stage of the reign and sway of God in the hearts and lives of men. One feels everywhere in the early accounts the throb and thrill of great expectation. The mirage is to become a pool, the highway for holy feet is to run over hill and valley, the trees are ready again to clap their hands, and there seems to be a touch of the marvellous and miraculous in many of the events they record. The wonder is that there is so much poise and restraint and not a greater outbreak of *Schwärmerei*, for they assumed that the lily, the symbol of the new era, had bloomed and that the " Seed " of God was born to usher in a new day. This intense faith is unmistakable to one who reads beneath the surface in the glowing words which come from the first flush of the Quaker movement. The later writers and compilers toned down the exuberance and marvel as much as they dared. They had themselves slowed down to a steadier pace, the glow had cooled away and they were not quite so sure that they were the bearers of a priceless hope for the world, but the evidence is clear enough that the " first Publishers of Truth ", as they called their early preachers, believed that they were in the true apostolic succession and had a glorious torch of light to transmit.

This faith that apostolic Christianity is being revived and restored is an ancient attitude of mind. George Fox is by no means the first to conceive himself to be commissioned for this task. Again and again in the twilight periods of Church History some man, in a burst of inspiration, has felt himself to be the chosen instrument of such a restoration. It is a natural idealizing bent of mind, and there are numerous texts in the New Testament which seem to eager readers to favour such hope and expectation. Many of the glowing " returns " to apostolic purity which history records seem to us in retrospect somewhat fantastic and abortive. There has often been a tendency to imitate some obvious or superficial aspect of primitive Christianity rather than to grasp comprehensively the central meaning and spirit of the truth and life that came through the great Galilean. But even if the restorer were ever so great a spiritual genius and had ever so wonderful depth of life and comprehensiveness of spirit, he could hardly succeed in effecting a " return " to the primitive model or in " restoring " the Church of the first century. Religious movements do not go backward ; they go forward. In order to " restore " the apostolic Church, we should need to " restore " the mental outlook, the intellectual conceptions, the sentiments, habits and civilization of that time. Religion is not something apart from life and thought which can be dropped into an age from some other epoch and be superimposed upon its own peculiar life and thought. We can go back, as we constantly need to do, to the headwaters of our faith and revisualize and revalue that great Life who is the source of our Christianity. We need to refresh our minds and our hearts by closer contact with the men who planted and watered the seed from which the great Igdrasil tree of the ages has grown. We need to renew our inspiration and deepen our impression of the spiritual conquest and the vital construction of those first apostolic men. Every line of their writing is precious, every glimpse of their lives is important, every lesson we can learn from their problems is worth all the labour it costs us to win it. But we cannot recover " the tender grace of a day that is dead ". The feel of their experience is for ever different from ours. Their thoughts are not our thoughts. The same words mean one thing to them and another thing to us. Edens can never be restored nor can apostolic Churches. The best we can do is to make our new Eden and build the Church of the Spirit as near as possible perhaps like the pattern in the Mount, but in each age suited to the climate and atmosphere of the time, and the kind of Church best fitted to produce the truest life and service. We shall not, then, expect to find in the Quaker movement a replica of the first century. It is not that. If those early Quaker builders thought it was that, they were mistaken. What they did do, and do very well, was to lay hold upon certain basic principles and spiritual ideals which were admirably suited to the temper and trend of the modern world. There is something truly *prophetic* in the creative work of these seventeenth-century builders, and we must try to see what their fundamental ideas were.

What they did was to insist that religion is something that begins within in the soul of man. They passed over, as Copernicus did, to a new centre. This change of centre underlay Luther's new interpretation of faith, but Luther failed to go all the way through with his reforming idea. He stopped midway. What Friends aimed to do was to ground religion for ever upon an inherent relation between God as living Spirit and the elemental spiritual nature of man. Religion, they believed, does not rise outside and flow in ; it springs up inside and flows out. It is not primarily concerned with books, documents, creeds or institutions. It is rather concerned with the awakening of a divine urge in the utmost deeps of the self. Man is, literally, "incurably religious". It is impossible to be fully completely *man* without the right culture and development of that inner capacity for God which is as much a feature of our being as is our appetite for mother's milk. It is true, no doubt, that many persons "go through life" without being consciously aware of their high endowment, they accumulate "things", live in their outside world, "make good", as they and their friends suppose, and never show any real sign of what I am calling "religion". But it could probably be shown, as George Fox showed many a man of that easy class in his day, that such persons have had plenty of "intimations" of their high possibilities and have passed many "crises" when they almost found the other slope of their great divide, which would have carried them far over in a very different direction of life and would have brought them finally to a very different sea of exit. Appetites of all sorts are subtle, delicate things and can, at their budding time, be easily turned out of their normal course and become altered into something quite unlike their primitive aim. This is peculiarly so with those *deeper* inward hungers of ours. The *push for the beyond* is always there in us, but it may take any one of many directions, and temporary expedients may wean us from its native drive for eternal satisfactions.

Anyway, whether psychologically right or wrong in the premises, Friends staked their whole case on the inherent religious capacity of the soul. Their position in this matter was plainly influenced, directly or indirectly, by the testimony of the mystics to a divine spark, or apex, in the soul. They were still more definitely under the spell of the great words of John's Gospel about " the Light that lighteth every man that cometh into the world ", and " the Spirit that guides into all the truth ", and the phrase in I Peter of a birth " of the incorruptible seed by the word of God ". They had, too, their own convincing immediate experience which seemed to them to reveal a Light from heaven breaking in on their darkness.

It is useless now to debate the question whether that divine trait belongs essentially to the human soul or is something supernaturally added to it as a free act of God. I suppose there is little doubt that many of the early Friends held the latter view, certainly Robert Barclay did. It was an age that did its thinking with pretty sharp dualisms. There had been then very little real adjustment to the revolutionary theory of Copernicus. There has been even yet very little attempt to think through what is involved in the new conception of the sky, which logically is more destructive of old theology than the theory of evolution is. In the seventeenth century, most people still thought of the sky as a crystalline dome, of heaven as " up there ", of God as dwelling yonder, of everything " here below ", including the human soul, as belonging to the " natural sphere ", and, consequently, as undivine and sundered from God. Whatever *partook of the divine*, and was to *operate spiritually*, must on this theory come from beyond the chasm which divided the two sundered spheres, and, therefore, be " a supernatural agent ". We do not, most of us, I hope, think that way now, though assuredly some do still think in such terms. We find it easy and normal to think of God as immanent, i.e. as living within our world, though I hope none of us would be satisfied with an immanence which confused God with the universe and identified Him with it. We find divine traces and pointings everywhere in the so-called natural sphere. We cannot *explain* anything without introducing more than we can see or touch. Time is only a " fragment " of the eternity in which it has its meaning. Evolution is not " evolution " unless the life series is significantly unfolding and really going somewhere. All the little arcs presuppose a greater curve, and least of all can we explain the soul, with its passion for truth and beauty and goodness, with its moral imperatives, and its intimations clear of wider scope, without presupposing some kind of junction with God.

These first Friends who *trembled* with a consciousness of God's nearness to them, and who rightly got the name of " quakers ", were in no doubt about the main fact. There was One nearer to them than breathing who " spoke to their condition ". They felt the healing of God drop upon their souls. The whole creation had a new smell. They were " moved " to their tasks. They had dealing not with flesh and blood but with Spirit. They were called out from the plough and shop to enter upon a high commission. *They* at least had no doubt that " something in man " was in direct correspondence with God. They therefore eliminated mediators and seconds, and insisted upon the direct way and that which was first.

It may be contended that they overstressed the direct approach and undervalued methods of mediation. It is true that we finite beings, with our grave limitations and with the feebleness of our powers of initiative, greatly need secondary helps and are bound to look outside ourselves and beyond ourselves for concrete interpretations of the way of life. There is no doubt that we have inherent capacity for appreciating beauty, but the cultivation of fine tastes is a slow and difficult achievement and calls for the guidance of experts and for the use of the accumulated gains of the ages. In no field of life does one leap to the height of attainment without drawing upon the wisdom and skill of many forerunners and many contemporaries. If religion were an isolated trait, a thing apart, a something mysteriously superadded to life without correlating with the processes of it, then perhaps we might think of it as " coming " without any mediations and describable steps, but real religion is not something detached from the rest of life and therefore it should grow and develop as all life does. We may quite well admit then that these Friends underestimated the importance of secondary helps and outward guidance.

What they were concerned about, however, with a concern that was absolutely sound, was that the autonomy of the soul should be protected and safeguarded. They had seen enough, and more than enough, of outside compulsion in religious matters. It had been thought of too long as something in the possession and control of a historic institution, something infallibly preserved and held and something to be transmitted ready-made to the new recipient. It was this theory that the Quaker challenged and denied in behalf of the inherent rights of the soul. The soul itself, as even Carthaginian Tertullian admitted, " when it comes to itself, as out of a surfeit, or a sleep, or a sickness and attains something of its natural soundness, speaks of God ", and has an experience to tell. This theory of the soul was, of course, not absolutely new. It did, however, run flatly counter to the main current of the Reformation. It was positive heresy in the ears of the followers of Luther and Calvin, and it had no standing with the guardians of orthodoxy anywhere. It seemed out of line with the general prevailing conception of the " fall ". It met the pessimism of depravity with a rival optimism about human potentiality. The Puritan saw in man a wreck like that of a ship hopelessly stranded on a reef of jagged rock. The Quaker saw in him a wreck, if wreck at all, like that of the buds in spring, burst from within by the warm sun, after having been tightly sealed all winter against sleet and storm, wrecked indeed, and by the push and power of a deeper, larger life working within and preparing for vast future possibilities.

We have here, then, a type of Christianity which begins with experience rather than with dogma. Luther, again, took this position in his great battle-documents which were written in the years that followed the nailing up of his Theses. His saving *faith* is an inward attitude based upon first-hand experience. It is " an active, powerful thing ", " a deliberate confidence in the grace of God ", which makes a man " joyous and intrepid " and ready to die for it " a thousand deaths ". But as the Reformation proceeded, the old dogma of the Church assumed an ever-increasing importance and in the end doctrine was raised to a status which overpassed anything known in the mediæval Church. In fact, the acceptance and maintenance of sound doctrines became the essential condition of salvation. *Faith* ceased to be an active, powerful attitude of will ; it became synonymous with " belief ". The Church was built up around its doctrine and it took on the aspect of a fort or garrison constructed to defend its saving doctrine. This position became an obsession. Christian bodies divided and subdivided over abstruse points of belief. Wars were fought. Nations were wrecked. Humanity was forgotten. The spirit of the divine Founder was ignored in the determination to maintain at all costs the " sacred " decision of some synod. The way of life inaugurated by the Crucified weighed as almost nothing in comparison with the only true theory of the atonement which some man had formulated.

George Fox called all these formulated beliefs " notions ". He pointed out that they could all be believed, adopted, held and defended without cleansing, purifying or transforming one's heart in the very least. They were thundered from pulpits and received with " amens ", but the lives of the affirming congregation seemed to him but little altered thereby. These things appeared to him to occupy a similar position to that which circumcision occupied in St. Paul's mind and which " Works " held in Luther's thought. One could carry all these matters through to the very end and still be the same unchanged person. " Not circumcision, but a new creation ", is St. Paul's demand. " Not works, but a discovery by faith that God is for us ", is Luther's message. " Not the holding of notions, but an inward transforming experience of God ", is George Fox's word of life.

The important point is that one must begin with something *vital*, and not with something merely formal and forensic. The essential transaction is not outside but inside. We want to get across from an old self to a new self, from an old way of living to a new way of living. It often, perhaps usually, involves a change of ideas. We cannot ignore here the crucial significance of right thinking. Many a person fails to be " saved ", to get his feet on the highway of salvation, because he is tied up with a muddled system of thinking. He goes on " believing what isn't so ". He is trying to live on what is in fact a stock of errors about the eternal nature of things, and he cannot " prosper " as he would if he knew the truth and had the freedom and power of it. Fox, and the Friends who have followed him, have always stood like adamant for the everlasting significance of *truth*. They do not encourage slip-shod thinking as though it made no difference. They induce no one to suppose that there is some inward magic which will save us from the effects of calling black white in matters that have to do with the soul's welfare.

What they disapprove is the tendency to set up as standards of faith and as essentials of salvation ancient doctrines which have been adopted in controversial gatherings, which deal often with issues very different from those *alive* in our day, and which carry on the mental outlook and intellectual attitudes of centuries long past and outgrown. Religious truth must grow like all truth. It must spring out of living experience. It must fit the convictions and aspirations of the time. It must be current coin. Whatever is proved and verified is thereby orthodox. We owe immense debts to past centuries in which heroic souls fought their valiant fight for the truth and passed it on to us. But their loyal devotion and their glimpse of truth do not settle our issues or relieve us from personal decision and present-day action. No manna for the soul can be permanently kept over, and discoveries of truth or light cannot be " passed on " in sealed containers.

Experience, then, is the Quaker's starting-point. This light must be *my* light, this truth must be *my* truth, this faith must be my very own faith. The key that unlocks the door to the spiritual life belongs not to Peter, or to some other person, as an official. It belongs to the individual soul, that finds the light, that discovers the truth, that sees the revelation of God and goes on living in the demonstration and power of it. For this there is no substitute. One can be saved with but very little theology, but no one can be saved who does not personally *want* to be saved, who does not himself *intend* to be saved and who does not meet the grace of God with an inward swing of *affirmation.*

Perhaps no Christian body has ever made more than the Friends have of the continued life and presence of Christ. It is a central idea in St. Paul's Epistles. There are well-known passages in the Synoptic Gospels promising Christ's continued presence ; for example, " Where two or three are gathered in my name, there am I in the midst " ; " Lo, I am with you always ". There were, too, experiences in the life of the early Church reported in *Acts* which indicate that assembled groups did on occasion rise to a vivid consciousness of His real presence. But it remained for the great Ægean apostle to give the truth and the experience their most complete expression. He rests his assurance of the living Christ, not upon a single vision which occurred to him on the Damascus read, but upon a continuous experience of resident life and power, thought of as Christ living and working within him. In St. Paul's experience Christ has become a living, operating Spirit as truly *present* in his own inner self as the heat and power of the sun are present where the roots are being quickened and the buds open to a new life. " He lives in me ", " I can do all things through Christ who energizes me." The energy to which St. Paul refers with great variety of phrase is always conceived as an actual spiritual power, which he feels " working " within him and transforming him from one stage of attainment to the next higher one—" from glory to glory ". " The *power* of the resurrection " is the energy of the living Christ, changing him from a dying man to a triumphant and immortal person until finally " that which is mortal is swallowed up of life."

George Fox rediscovered this idea and this experience almost as completely as Luther rediscovered St. Paul's doctrine of " the righteousness of God by faith ". Luther's doctrine at first was certainly vital, but it slid very easily over into a forensic transaction, or even into something magical. The Reformation tended to drift away from *experience of vital energies* to *a sacred theory of salvation*. Fox swung back strongly to the vital aspects of St. Paul's faith and experience. In this tendency he had a great forerunner in Jacob Boehme, who laid all his emphasis on the inward power of salvation and who felt a positive horror of forensic and magical theories of salvation. In his failure to find help and guidance from the ministers of his day, at the end of his agonizing search, Fox records this illuminating experience : " When all my hopes in all men were gone, so that I had nothing outwardly to help me, nor could I tell what to do, then, oh then, I heard a voice which said, ' There is one, even Christ Jesus that can speak to thy condition ', and when I heard it my heart did leap for joy."

This is the turning-point in Fox's life—his Damascus vision—and what happens is that he finishes with theories and notions and is done with man-constructed schemes and finds a real presence, a force of spiritual life, operating within himself, " closer than breathing ", inwardly felt. It is a sample experience. The rest of his life is marked throughout by a continuation of similar occurrences more or less vivid and effective. What he calls " Seed " and " Light " and " Spirit " is in his mind nothing less than a continuation of the life of Christ, operating within as a resident presence and a vital power. He would have endorsed the bold words of Angelus Silesius :

> Wird Christus tausendmal
> Zu Bethlehem geboren
> Und nicht in dir : du bleibst
> Noch ewiglich verloren.[1]

Friends have not always realized the full significance of this idea. They have had their slumps and slides toward forensic thinking and artificial methods of salvation, but their own prophets and spiritual leaders in all generations of the Quaker movement have been " vitalists " and not scheme-purveyors. They have called men to a way of life. They have felt that theory and doctrines are " sounding brass and clanging cymbals " compared with the actual formation of the spirit of Christ in the fibre and structure of the inner life. The other way is easy, and this path no doubt seems slow and painful. It is vastly easier to take photographs than it is to paint the likeness and character of a person with brush on canvas, but only in this latter way does the deeper life come out for the beholder. It is easy to say words and to quote formulas,

> [1] Had Christ a thousand times
> Been born in Bethlehem
> But not in thee, thy sin
> Would still thy soul condemn.

E

but life comes to its full glory only when a finite man like one of us becomes the living organ of the life of God.

If any one supposes that Friends have inclined to be "humanists" and to assume that man is so inherently good that he can lift himself by his own belt into a life of consummate truth and beauty, he has not yet caught the deeper note of the Quaker faith. Friends have always exalted Christ. They have been as eager as any Christians to know the facts of the gospels and to have sound, clear knowledge of the events in the life of the Jesus of history. They have been very desirous to see vividly and effectively that wonderful person who lived and preached and healed, and helped and loved and died and rose again. They have not usually blurred or slighted the outward life lived in the frame of time and space. But, like St. Paul, they are most concerned with the inward Christ. He is the source of their life and power. The Quaker poet, John Greenleaf Whittier, has finely expressed for the whole fellowship what He means as a living presence :

> Warm, sweet, tender, even yet
>   A present help is He ;
> And faith has still its Olivet,
>   And love its Galilee.
>
> The healing of His seamless dress
>   Is by our beds of pain ;
> We touch Him in life's throng and press
>   And we are whole again.
>
> Through Him the first fond prayers are said
>   Our lips of childhood frame,
> The last low whispers of our dead
>   Are burdened with His name.

Our Lord, and Master of us all!
    Whate'er our name or sign,
We own thy sway, we hear thy call,
    We test our lives by thine.

The only other point which needs to be added to this account of the Quaker type of faith is the effect of such views upon the basis of authority. This question of authority is always a serious and urgent one. The leaders of the Reformation found themselves inevitably confronted with it. What is the test and final criterion of faith? If one breaks with an ancient authoritative system, there is no way to escape the necessity of restating some new basis of authority. If one promulgates what he calls "truth", he is bound to tell us why he considers it to be more than opinion, and what in the last analysis is his ground of *must be so*.

At first, authority was felt to rest upon superior power, though it is hardly likely that authority could ever be quite reduced to an equality with power or force. There is always a mental fringe of awe attaching to the attitude of response to authority. But in the earliest stage it is superior power which makes a command or an announcement carry weight and win obedience. Gradually we pass over to the authority of custom, tradition and venerable antiquity. The principle of habit is everywhere an operative force. The past rolls up, like a rolling snowball, and accumulates energy and power. We want to repeat what we have always done; so do groups of people, so do races. The little child wants the same story over again. We prefer to live in the same house, to sit in the same seat, to use the same language—we tend all the time to mechanize our ways of doing things. The past transmits its momentum. This is peculiarly so in the sphere of religion. The religious habits of a long line of ancestors become sacred and authoritative in their own right. What they did, what they thought, comes to us with a halo and a dim magnificence. It has been tried, too, and tested through long experience ; it *works*, and incidentally it saves us of the later time the necessity of creating something new ! Everywhere one turns it is possible to find evidence of the authority of the past—what our restless young people call " the authority of the dead hand ".

There is another kind of authority which challenges both these other types and in the end " takes their crown ". The authority of facts, the authority of the laboratory, the authority of demonstration seems to us to-day to be the last word in the matter. When Galileo proved by positive demonstration that the earth *moved* on its axis and around the sun, it was useless for any organization however powerful or for any dogma however hoary with age to attempt to change the *truth* of that demonstrated fact.

We come up at last against the *eternal nature of things*. There is a *must* written on the face of the universe and in the mind of man. The laboratory teacher with his test tube and equations speaks with an authority which any preacher envies. He does not raise his voice nor pound his desk—he quietly reveals the facts and they produce *an inevitable conviction*. There is an inherent must attaching to the nature of truth when it once is discovered.

Friends have always approved this last kind of authority and have endeavoured to build their religious faith upon the inherent authority of truth. They come back for their basis to the test of experience— to the laboratory of life. They would not endorse the view that a position is necessarily sound and right and true *because* it comes to the individual's consciousness with a powerful sense of conviction and with a coercive " urge ". To be cock-sure is not always to be right. The Friends lay much emphasis upon the importance of testing one's *insight* by convincing the spiritual group of fellow-members of its truth-quality, but they put much more importance on the test of life. Is the conviction, the insight, the urge one that fits in well with the tested laws and principles of life and character ? Will it construct a richer life, a holier disposition ? Will it build a better group and form a nobler spirit ?

We do not have here the quick and easy methods of test which belong to a physical laboratory. We cannot weigh and measure with the same exactness. Our demonstration is slower and more halting, but after all it is *demonstration*. The thing is *so*, because the eternal nature of things backs it and because it contributes to that highest thing the universe is making—a spiritual person and a better world.

CHAPTER IV

THE STRUCTURE AND METHOD OF THE SOCIETY OF FRIENDS

FROM what I have said in the two previous chapters, it will be seen that we are dealing with a type of religion which may appropriately be called mystical. The word is a loose and fluid one. It has various meanings. I am using it to signify that God is essentially a God who reveals and communicates Himself, and man is essentially a being with spiritual capacities and therefore susceptible within himself to the " radio-activity " of the life of God. The division of the universe into a hard and fast two-world system—an undivine half, down here, where we inhabit, and a supernaturally divine half, yonder, where He dwells in remote and solitary splendour—is a crude and mediæval way of thinking. It is perhaps a slander on the Middle Ages to call that theory " mediæval ", for the wisest men of the Middle Ages thought of God as being " as near to us as we are to ourselves ".

The Quakers felt convinced, and still are convinced, by their own experience that this tiny rill of our own individual life somehow, somewhere is conjunct with the Ocean of Spirit, whose tides flow back upon us and let us feel the sea-beat of the eternal reality. The circulation runs both ways. There is a double-search. We transcend our little fragmentary selves and try

to make our contacts and to establish our correspondence with the Tidal-Sea, and the Central Life at
the heart of things is forever pressing in toward us.
There are rivers, like Abana and Pharpar, " Rivers of
Damascus ", which never reach an ocean and never
feel a tide. They flow out into the sands of an arid
desert and are lost in the marshes which their own
waters make. There may, of course, be human lives
like that, which connect only with the shallow cistern
of their inland exits. The Quaker does not believe
that. He holds a working faith that we all touch a
deeper Life and are within hail of " that immortal Sea
that brought us hither ".

That being so, the religion of the Quaker is primarily
concerned with the culture and development of the
inward life and with this direct correspondence with
God. The Quaker genius, if he has any unique genius,
will quite naturally be displayed in contriving ways
and methods for furthering this primary quest. Organization and external systems will not interest him very
much. He will take most naturally and most kindly
to ways of worship that encourage and assist mystical
experience. This tendency is clearly seen in the entire
form and structure of *the Quaker meeting for worship*,
which is on its deepest side the central feature of
Quakerism. The meeting has as little organization as
is consistent with order and group-procedure. The
room in which the meeting is held is usually very plain
and simple. There is nothing to attract attention or to
distract the mind. There are no loud colours, the
walls and the seats being very quietly toned. There is
usually no desk, no focal point from which special
exercises may be expected to emerge. In many meeting
houses, there are some seats, slightly raised in front,

facing the main congregation. Here those may sit who are most likely to take some vocal part in the meeting. In some instances, the seats are arranged in a square with raised seats on at least three sides of the house, so that *expectation* will not be turned in any one particular direction. In meetings of this type, there is no fixed order of service, no chosen leader, no august figure. The meeting is a spiritual democracy, and the messages on any given occasion, if there are any spoken ones, may come from any person there.

The meeting will usually not begin with any words, though there is no unvarying rule about it. As the meeting is held primarily for worship and communion, and not for talk, it is apt to begin, as one would expect, with a time of hush and quiet. What Rudolf Otto has called the " numinous " experience is here in evidence ; that is, the experience of divine presence. There is a moved and overbrimming state of mind. It is not exactly " thinking ", not perhaps quite " meditation ". It is what the old Friends used to call *centring down.* There is a unification of the interior life, in which the rational and emotional powers, together with the bended energies of will purpose, are fused into a waiting and expectant attitude. At the best, there is a corporate sense of overbrooding presence, a feeling of awe and wonder, and a straining forward of spirit to join co-operatively with the invading Life and Spirit. It is a mystical group-experience of a mild and unecstatic type. Each helps all, and all help each. Healing, vitalizing currents seem to flow from life to life. The heart burns with joy and often faces shine with a light from within. I have seen quiet tears on such occasions course down cheeks of men, made though they were of stern stuff, who were seldom ever seen to weep elsewhere. When one is in Damascus, he often hears the currents of invisible submerged rivers running underneath the streets of the city, and somewhat so one feels in these meetings at their best a tide of living Spirit flowing underneath the hushed and gathered group. Other churches have other ways of assisting the individual in this momentous business of worshipping God and of coming into vital contact with the spiritual environment of the soul. The Friends for three centuries have been experts in the way of silence, the way of wonder, as it has been happily called.

Their testimony is peculiarly needed at the present time. Recollection, meditation, concentration, unification are almost lost arts. The world hardly knows any longer how to centre down ; how, in the midst of noise and confusion, to hush all voices except the still small voice ; how, in the whirl and turmoil of ever-shifting scenes and sights, to cultivate *the single eye, the eye that sees the invisible*. The world needs, I say, those who practise this rare and supreme art of communion, those who " have ears to hear what the Spirit saith ". Friends themselves have still much to learn in this field. I have called them " experts ", but they are experts in much the sense that Galen and Hippocrates were experts in medicine. They were experts when compared with the herb-doctor or the purveyor of charms and spells. But when you compare them with Sir William Osler, they shrink to small dimensions as experts. Friends have merely kept alive a sound method. They have maintained a practice which is on right lines—their contribution, however, is but a firefly's light when contrasted with the blaze of sunlight which the jaded world needs to heal and refresh its tired spirit.

The meeting for worship is, however, not all silence. The silence is preparation. One listens before one speaks. There is a quickening power in *living* silence, though, of course, dead silence tends to kill out freshness and spontaneity. Where the temperature and atmosphere of the group are right, the one who prays or speaks is not just a solitary individual saying words. He becomes in some real sense a voice for the co-operating group. There is more in his words than he *consciously* knows or *explicitly* thinks out. There is a certain team-effect, a cumulative power, such as one often sees when the expectant attitude of an audience in some moment of crisis suddenly raises an orator to a height of eloquence which he could never reach by himself and perhaps never does reach on any other occasion.

The Quakers, in the long quietistic period of the eighteenth century and the first half of the nineteenth, were under a hampering theory, which was not really consistent with the deeper truth of their mystical principle, that each person should go to meeting with an " empty mind ", as they called it. It was assumed on the part of each one that there should be no preparation, no thought of any topic, no expectation of making vocal utterance. Whatever words were to be uttered were to be spontaneously and divinely " given " at the moment. The speaker must be *moved*, specifically called out, impelled, constrained, with a woe upon him if he did not rise to his feet. And then his message was to be not so much " inspired " as " dictated ", so that the one who spoke or prayed acted as an ancient oracle did—transmitting what was mysteriously given. The Montanists insisted that their " prophets " should be passive like the lyre which is struck by the musician's finger or by his plectrum, the holy Spirit being in this case the musician and the plectrum. The quietistic Friends took pretty much that view of ministry. The theory had disastrous effects for many reasons, the most serious reason being that it involved a fundamental misunderstanding both of the nature of God and the nature of man and their mutual relationship. It was the old double-world theory come back again—God and man sundered. It showed, too, a profound misconception of human personality. It implied that God could use a person best when he was a hollow tube. It indicated that the inward gains, accumulations, and riches of a life-time of experience are of no value, and must be " suppressed " before God can work advantageously. It was a dull, flat, mechanical view which fitted the climate of the eighteenth century. Fortunately, the best ministers of the period rose in practice far above their theory, and, while holding it, transcended it, though it did clip their wings and shorten their range and circuit.

It doomed many meetings to almost perennial silence. They did not have in their group persons who ever had such " movings ". It naturally tended to limit ministry to one peculiar type of person, the psychic, prophetic type, i.e. to persons possessed of peculiar subconscious traits and capacities who felt themselves swept by impulses which they could not trace to their own conscious thoughts or contrivings. These sudden flashes of insight or flushes of truth seemed alone of divine origin, and if nobody among them had any such, then nothing would be said.

The idea behind all this was sound enough. They were endeavouring to eliminate what they would have

called " man-made " talk, " pumped up " addresses,
cut-and-dried—especially *dried*—deliverances and com-
munications. The eighteenth century was very fond
of the phrase " creaturely activity ", which meant
doing something, by word or deed, which was " out of
the life ", which lacked vitality, which was devoid of
Spirit and Power, and had only a superficial and artificial origin in some individual's desire to be busy, to
be " doing things ". Friends were trying to get as far
away from that sort of thing as possible. They wanted
a ministry that was fresh, vital, divinely initiated,
anointed with the oil of grace, in a word " spiritual ",
and not mechanical. They felt that if God was to
come in, man must go out ; if a contribution was to
be spiritual, it must not have any human element.
" Divine " and " human " were *alternative* terms, not
correlative and contributory truths. We have come,
I hope, to see that wherever spiritual operations are
manifested, both God and man are working together,
are conjunct, as the convex and concave sides of a
curve must be joined before there can be a curve.

With this new psychology of man and this true
interpretation of God, the ancient practice of Quaker
worship admirably fits. God does not need to come
from somewhere else to find us and to meet with us—
" Does the fish soar to find the ocean, does the eagle
plunge to find the air ? " But the human spirit does
need to become centred, organized, sensitized. Men
lived thousands of years in the world before they knew
that electrical energy filled all space and formed the
uninterrupted environment of every person. It touches
us at every point. It is closer than the air we breathe.
It penetrates bones and viscera. But it breaks through
and is revealed only where matter is so organized as

to let it come through and operate. The dynamo reveals it, though the unorganized and unconstructed pieces of metal which compose the dynamo give no hint, in their separate state, that electric forces are near at hand.

Human personality is best adapted of any reality known to us in our universe for the revelation of God. There are certain aspects of the divine life and character which cannot, so far as we can see, be revealed in any other way. If God is Spirit, then only spirit can fully reveal Him. If He is love, than only some one who can rise to an appreciation of love, and can at the same time himself exhibit love, can either grasp or express the nature of such a divine Being. The hush, the silence, the concentration, the expectancy, the group-co-operation, the wonder, awe and reverence all tend to prepare for the great experience, and all help to make the meeting a time of inspiration and correspondence. And we may say, I think, that in such a quickened atmosphere, the person who is to speak is brought to his best state and condition for an effective message, and the rest of the group are, at the same time, attuned for the reception of it. The ideal meeting is one in which no person speaks at great length, but the torch is passed from hand to hand, and three or four speak, harmoniously interpreting the same general theme.

The business meetings of the Society of Friends are graded upwards from a small local group which meets once a month to a large inclusive body which meets annually and is called the " Yearly Meeting ". The Monthly Meeting may include only one congregation, or it may include two or three congregations. It is the only body which can receive or dismiss members. It appoints " Elders ", who are selected to look after the spiritual welfare of the congregations to which they belong, to counsel and advise those who speak in ministry and to bear the deeper interests and concerns of the meeting on their hearts. These " Elders " have had an important part in the deeper spiritual life of the Society of Friends. They have not usually been bearers themselves of public messages. They are not selected because of their gifts as speakers. They have rather been notable for their quiet wisdom, their penetration, their depth of character, the weight of their judgment and the convicting power of their fragrant lives. They have to a marked degree incarnated the spirit and ideals of Quakerism. They have perhaps in the past exercised more influence in the way of restraint than as a constructive force. They were quick to discern where ministry failed or missed the mark. They were not quite so gifted with insight to see the budding powers in young speakers, to guide the fresh adventurer with wise counsel and to draw out latent possibilities by words of encouragement. In short, they were better at the brakes than they were for the application of the spurs ! The Monthly Meeting also appoints " Overseers ", who are selected to manage the pastoral work of the congregations to which they belong. They have wide functions and a great variety of services. They visit members who are in trouble and need the spiritual support of the fellowship, they have the care and oversight of " the daily walk and conversation " of the members, they look after the moral and social interests of the body, and, in a general way, they do those things which in most churches would be managed by a rector, a curate or a pastor. It is another instance of the democratic tendency of Quakerism. They draw as many persons as possible into the service of the group, and make as many members as possible *responsible* for the life of the whole. This business of shepherding the flock is complicated and delicate. Too much of it is almost as fatal as too little. It is a fine art, and, like most things, is done best by those who have a genius for it, at least a gift for it. It is a gift, however, which does not necessarily go with the preaching gift and it may be found, in fact often is found, in the lives of ordinary and unofficial persons. Friends have often done excellent pastoral work through their "overseers", and again, in other communities, it has been done negligently and ineffectively. The important point to emphasize is *this* : that in all religious matters, as many members as possible should be drawn into active service and made to feel personal responsibility for the life of the church and for the advancement of truth. In this respect, the Quaker experiment has had a real value and is a positive contribution.

Above the Monthly Meeting is the Quarterly Meeting, which meets, as the name implies, four times in the year. It includes a group of Monthly Meetings and transacts the business which concerns the mutual welfare and interests of them all. It also prepares business for the Yearly Meeting. This latter meeting includes the members of many Quarterly Meetings and is the highest legislative body for a whole country, or for an extensive section of country. In Great Britain there is a single Yearly Meeting, another one in Ireland, and in America there are altogether twenty-nine such meetings, some of which are very small and are composed of Friends who have " separated " from other bodies.

A few words perhaps ought to be written on the unhappy and disastrous " separations " in American

Quakerism. The first one of importance occurred in Philadelphia in 1827, when the Friends of Pennsylvania and New Jersey divided into two " branches ", popularly known as " Orthodox " and " Hicksite ". It is not easy to label the points of difference between them, since there were a great many factors involved in the controversy and a large variety of motives and influences were in operation. The strain and tension came from two strong tendencies of the period, one in the direction of a powerful evangelical emphasis, and the other in the direction of a freer and more liberal type of thought and with increased emphasis on the inner light of the individual. The Orthodox group represented the former and the Hicksite party—led originally by Elias Hicks, of Jericho, on Long Island, New York—expressed the other tendency. The separation produced at the time much bitterness and ill-feeling, and eventually led to separations in six other Yearly Meetings.

In 1845 a second cleavage occurred, this time in New England. The lines were less clearly drawn than in the first division. The personal equation was more in evidence and petty issues were raised to far too great an importance. John Wilbur, of Westerly, Rhode Island, represented the conservative tendency in the struggle. He believed that he stood for the primitive, apostolic form of Quakerism as taught by George Fox and Robert Barclay, while his opponents were friends and followers of the distinguished English Friend, Joseph John Gurney, who was a powerful preacher, a Biblical scholar, an intense evangelical, and who seemed to John Wilbur to represent a " new " brand of Quakerism, out of harmony with that of the fathers and founders of the Society. There were sad scenes, with mistakes on both sides, and unfortunate events, and finally the division came. This break in New England led to other separations in Ohio, New York and Indiana, with a tiny one in Pennsylvania called "Primitive Friends", and later there came small separations of conservative Friends in Kansas, Iowa, Canada and North Carolina.

Thirteen American Yearly Meetings are joined in maintaining a Five Years Meeting, which transacts business for the larger corporate and spiritual interests of all these Yearly Meetings, stretching from Canada and New England across to the Pacific coast. The total membership in America—all bodies—is about 120,000 Friends. London Yearly Meeting, which includes Friends in Australia and on the continent of Europe, is somewhat over 20,000, and the Yearly Meeting in Ireland has a membership of over 2,000. There are consequently somewhat less than 150,000 Quakers in the world.

London Yearly Meeting maintains an extraordinary body known as the "Meeting for Sufferings". Originally it looked after the sufferings of Friends in the periods of severe persecution, but with the course of time, it has taken up the sufferings of the world and the moral and spiritual tasks that go with the relief of sufferings. There are similar meetings, known as the "Representative Meeting", in both Philadelphia Yearly Meetings, and all the other Yearly Meetings have various organizations for accomplishing the same ends.

One of the most interesting of all Quaker experiments in democracy is to be found in the method of transacting business in these various groups. Quaker meetings for business, like the meetings for worship, usually begin and end in silence. There is a period of solemn hush and preparation, sometimes followed by

F

vocal prayer, and an effort is made to have all the business conducted on the high spiritual plane that characterizes the meeting for worship. The clerk, who sits at the recording desk, is not a chairman in the parliamentary sense. No " motions " are made and " seconded ". No votes are taken. The clerk usually introduces business, though it may also be introduced by a committee, or by any member of the meeting who has a " concern " upon his mind, and naturally a large amount of business comes up from the minutes of the previous meeting. As soon as the business is clearly laid before the meeting, the speaking is free and open. Gradually a definite proposition emerges from the discussion and the speaking then focuses about this topic. The clerk's function is to keep the discussion definitely to the matter before the meeting and to decide whether there is unity of judgment enough to warrant a minute of conclusion. If there is, he proposes a minute which gathers up and expresses " the sense of the meeting ". The meeting is then asked whether it is satisfied with the statement. If there is unity, the matter is considered settled and a new subject is introduced. If, however, there is not substantial unity attained throughout the discussion, the decision is deferred. Sometimes the issue is postponed to the next meeting in the hope that time and reflection will ripen the project and deepen the comprehension of it. Usually it is put in the hands of a small committee which will, in the interim, gather information, study the project, re-formulate it and set it forth in clearer light so that the members at the next meeting may deal with it more intelligently. Then once more " the sense of the meeting " will be taken.

By this method, the rights of the " minority " are

not overlooked or neglected. In fact, there is no majority or minority; there is a group striving to arrive at unity. Everybody's judgment counts for what it is worth and *weighs* something if it helps to bring the group to clarity and decision. A speaker who obviously speaks without depth or insight, or who is minded to be stubborn and have his own selfish way, will usually carry little weight and will be discounted when " the sense of the meeting " is gathered up. The method is designed to secure a conclusion that is wiser than the judgment of any single man, a conclusion to which all have contributed and which gathers up the corporate wisdom of the body. It is not the same thing as " mob-mind " or " mass-thinking ". Instinct, emotion and unconscious psychic forces, especially imitation, are the great driving forces in producing these latter mass-results. The product is apt to be scaled down to the lower level of the intelligence of the group. The least common denominator wins. Men are swept along into decisions and acts of which they will be ashamed when the time for calm reflection comes.

The Quaker method, on the other hand, tends to draw out the highest and best that is potential to the group. It offers a fine opportunity for leadership. A wise proposition will carry weight. A calm, quiet, sincere presentation of one's view makes its impression. The discussion, in the atmosphere which usually prevails, puts everybody at his best for taking intelligent part. Ideas bud and sprout, fresh thoughts are born, the subject grows and gathers meaning, new aspects come to light, others are stimulated and the group may do, as it often does, a wiser and greater thing than anyone thought of when the matter was broached. More comes out than anybody puts in. Occasionally more comes forth than the total sum of what all put in—a whole that is greater than the sum of the parts. The noblest Quaker projects are thus often not the conception of some one person, but the living fruit of group-wisdom. It would naturally seem to some that too great respect is shown in this method to a minority that might easily frustrate the will of the larger fraction. This might, of course, happen in some instances. Usually, however, if the minority is intelligent and sincere, it will present matters that deserve serious consideration. The opposition wisely expressed and carefully presented will tend to modify an overhasty conclusion, and the final outcome will be much sounder than it would have been if it had not been held up and reconstructed. It does, one must admit, call for large charity and patience, for it often means the remote postponement of what had been believed to be near at hand. If, as sometimes happens, the minority opposition is plainly obstructive and ill-considered, if it springs out of pettiness and anti-group spirit, it will be treated as "without weight", and the better sense of the meeting will prevail.

The one thing that breaks down the method of business which I have been considering is the spirit of dissension, contention and disunity. The moment love, sympathy, the understanding mind, gentleness, forbearance and desire for unity vanish, this method fails to work. It is effective only when the temper and the atmosphere are right. It is a spiritual method and it more or less breaks down when the group ceases to be *spiritual*. Miss Follette, in her admirable book, *The New State*, has presented a somewhat similar type as a substitute for our unsatisfactory system of majority government. Her book is a positive and constructive contribution, but in this matter it would need more ideal conditions than we usually find in political parties and caucuses before we could secure the highest and united wisdom of all. Selfishness and self-seeking play havoc with methods which depend for success on the unity of the group.

The Quaker group in all meetings includes both men and women. In early times, the women held separate meetings apart by themselves and conducted their own affairs. But joint meetings have proved to be much more satisfactory. The Quaker women have always enjoyed a large degree of liberty and co-operation in all matters of a spiritual type, and there have frequently been outstanding leaders of this sex. At the present time, there is perfect equality of the sexes. They fit together,

> Like perfect music unto noble words.

CHAPTER V

FRIENDS AND THE SACRAMENTS

SACRAMENTS, or at least sacramental ideas, are as old as human history. Primitive peoples have frequently, in fact, almost universally, believed in the possibility of participating in the life of a god by eating or drinking something intimately associated with the god, something belonging to him, or something representing him in likeness or symbol. It has been well nigh universal, too, for men of primitive races to suppose that they could take over into themselves the traits and the powers of the animals that they ate, and in cases where tribes have indulged in cannibalism, they have usually assumed that they could, by eating a great chieftain or a hero-leader, attain the noble qualities of the man of whom they partook.

The mystery religions which flourished for many centuries in Greece, and which rose to a place of vast importance throughout the Greco-Roman world in the first century of our era, gave a unique significance to sacraments of initiation and sacraments of participation in the life of some hero-god. It is unnecessary here for the moment to raise the question whether the mystery religions of Greece had an important influence in shaping the developments of Christian sacraments in the apostolic period. There are excellent scholars on both sides of the question. There can hardly be any doubt, however, in the mind of a careful historical student that they did, in any case, have a profound later influence. But whether direct influence can be traced or not, the fact remains that the sacramental idea was practically universal in the religious habits and practices of those who came into the Christian Church from the pagan religions of the far-flung Roman empire. We may further, I think, take it as a sound working principle that there must be some deep truth and reality attaching to a method of communion which is almost as universal as religion is and which is as old, and at the same time as new, as human nature.

Friends are popularly supposed to have taken a radical attitude of negation toward the sacraments of the historic Church and to have entirely eliminated them. That attitude, however, applies in truth only to the *external* rite and practice, not to the inner experience which is at the heart of every genuine sacrament of life. The spiritual reformers of the sixteenth and seventeenth centuries, from whom the Friends are historically sprung, wanted to build a spiritual and invisible Church rather than a visible one, and they were afraid of machinery, officialism and all set routine and performance of an external sort. They were interested in everything that promoted the inner life and developed the spirit of a person, but they felt almost no interest in organization or system as such. They wanted the impossible—a spirit without a body to be its organ. William Dell, Master of Gonville and Caius College, Cambridge, a contemporary of George Fox, and one of the finest of the English spiritual reformers, wrote: " The truth must eat out the ceremony, and the substance the sign ; the more the baptism of Christ comes in, the more the baptism with water will go out ;

the ministry of the Son shall swallow up the ministry of the servant, as the sunlight doth the moonlight. The baptism of fire shall devour the baptism of water, and Christ's spirit-baptism by degrees shall put an end to water-baptism."

The Friends inherited much of that same preference for the inward as against the outward. They saw that their truth could not be preserved and propagated without some living organism to support and transmit the faith and experience which they had found and which were exceedingly precious to them, but they wanted the outward form and body to be as tenuous and uncrystallized as possible. They were resolved to have nothing set up and established which would be a substitute for the first-hand experience of the individual, or which would cool down into a merely recurrent practice or empty custom. They wanted every act and function of worship to be *in the life*, and to fit the inner spiritual needs of the soul.

The external sacramental practices which prevailed in the churches of the seventeenth century seemed to George Fox to have little inner meaning and but slender spiritual significance. They appeared to him, and to his " Children of the Light ", to have grown up through the dark ages and the middle ages very much as the creeds and doctrines had grown up. He classed them as " man-made " things and not as divinely ordained, as part of the load of superstitious accretion that had accumulated through the centuries. They seemed to him, eager as he was to preserve only *vital* functions, part of the dead wood of the " wilderness " period of the Church's life. He took the attitude which St. Paul had taken toward circumcision and which Luther had taken a century before toward

" sacred works ". But he had no thought of omitting or underestimating the spiritual reality for which the outward sacraments stood.

Fox and the members of his Society fed their minds on the Fourth Gospel. It had always been the favourite Gospel of the mystics and of the spiritual reformers. He drew upon its spiritual treasures as his forerunners had done. He brought to his reading of it no critical knowledge, which in any case did not exist in his century, and he possessed, of course, almost no historical insight about the formative period of the life of the Church. What he did do was to absorb the heart of the message and the way of life of this great book. He went to work to reproduce, as far as was possible in a later century, the spiritual Christianity of that Gospel. This Gospel omits all reference to the institution of the Supper on the night of the betrayal, and it distinctly declares that Jesus Himself did not baptize with water. It strongly contrasts the lesser form of baptism by water, which John practised, with the higher and essential baptism of the Spirit, which is included in Christ's commission.

Everywhere throughout this Gospel the emphasis is put on *qualities of life*, not on ritual observances. Instead of founding an ordinance on that last evening of His earthly life, the writer of this Gospel tells with depth and power how Christ bequeathed to His followers Truth and Peace and Love, which are unifying and spiritual legacies. He told them how to become His Friends—not by adopting a rite—but by loving as He had loved, and by entering heart and soul into the deeper purposes of His life and mission. John's Gospel tells with grace and simplicity how, at that last meeting with His disciples, Jesus girded Himself with a towel and went about from man to man washing the feet of His companions. This act of love and humility seems to have been purposely told by John in place of the Supper narrative of the other Gospels. He is consciously aiming to focus attention upon a spirit of love and service rather than upon a rite.

It may seem strange that the Friends, who were quick to notice John's substitution, did not adopt the sacrament of foot-washing, which obviously seems to be commanded in the passage. The answer is that they saw and felt and endeavoured to practise its deeper meaning, which might be easily missed in a set, repeated ceremony of washing feet. To them, the act was the revelation of a new and wonderful spirit of love. They saw revealed in it what was involved in being a true " Friend ". It was for them an acted parable of life. It flashed into their souls the real meaning of *service*, as humble, loving, sharing of life with others, the giving of self without any thought of return. It seemed to them that it would spoil the beautiful *act* to treat it as a rite and to repeat it in a routine and mechanical manner. What they wanted to do was to catch and transmit the same spirit which this act expressed, to feel that same love, and to show that same attitude of heart and mind.

That condition of life does not come by command. It cannot be produced to order. The very performance of a customary ritual of foot-washing may easily come to take the place of the deeper spiritual practice, may grow to be a substitute for it. Friends wisely took the great scene, as they took the breaking of the alabaster box of perfume, not as something to be repeated in literal form, but as something to be translated into the deeds and spirit of everyday life and applied in ordinary human relationships. Christ had said, My meat—My necessary food—is to do the will of Him that sent Me, and the true follower of Christ finds the food of his deepest life to be in doing what He did, in living and walking in His spirit.

The Friends found, as the spiritual reformers had found, the essential meaning of Christianity in the great discourse reported in the sixth chapter of John. It is generally recognized now that this discourse is throughout dealing with the deeper issues of the sacrament of the Supper, though the Friends, in the seventeenth century, quite naturally did not see that as they read the chapter. To them it told how a finite human being can participate in the divine Life, and that, for them, was the most important thing on earth or in any other world. The writer of the discourse is profoundly aware that external performances may easily become mechanical and superstitious, may lose all their power and vitality and, as a formal action, " profit nothing ". He, therefore, proceeds to present the deeper meaning of the mighty experience of communion. To " eat the flesh " and to " drink the blood " of Christ is declared to be the source and ground of all spiritual life. He wants it distinctly understood, however, that no external act of eating or drinking is adequate for that vital experience. It is of " no profit " to partake of food that feeds only the flesh. The thing that really matters is an inward participation in the Life of God as He is incarnated in Christ. " It is the spirit that quickeneth "—not bread, not flesh, not external performances. It is the assimilation of that divine Life into one's self that counts, the inward discovery of its spirit and power, the joyous reception of it as the spring and energy of one's own life. It seemed " a hard

saying " to those who listened. It turned many back
to their old ruts and grooves. It tested the chosen few
who, however, knew of " nowhere else to go ". But at
once it called for a new and higher way of living.
Christ was to be thought of not as a popular Messiah,
not merely as a heavenly visitor, but as one who in
human form like ourselves gives His Life to men to
live by, reveals a way of living which we can all enter,
manifests a love which we ourselves can share and is a
personal spirit that can become within us a vital force,
a living energy, so that His Life is propagated and
transmitted through us. Phillips Brooks, in one of
the short sermons in his *More Abundant Life*, beautifully puts this central truth : " We are to eat His
flesh. Now the flesh was the expression of the human
life of Jesus. It was in His incarnation that He
became capable of uttering those qualities in which
man might be like Him, which men might receive
from Him and take into themselves. Think of it.
God had stood before men from the first, and they had
looked with awe and adoration upon Him, throned
far above them. . . . What was there in the Deity
that could repeat itself in man ? Not His majesty,
not omnipotence and omniscience, surely. . . . Then
came the incarnation. Here was God in the flesh. . . .
It was the incarnate God ; it was God in the flesh that
was to enter into man. That was the flesh we were to
eat, and by which we were to live."

It was some such general view of Christ's teaching in
the Fourth Gospel which made the Quakers feel that
life, and not the performance of rites, constituted the
heart of the religion of the great Galilean. No less
emphatic and impressive to their minds was the teaching
of this same Gospel in reference to the way of *entrance*

upon the new life. The third chapter of the Gospel deals with this new step with the same depth and spiritual insight that are so evident in the chapter on participation through eating and drinking the life and spirit of Christ. The problem in the third chapter is the way of entrance into the kingdom of God. Once more, as in the sixth chapter, there is an obvious reference, in the use of the word *water*, to the ritual practice of the Church, though the Quaker reader did not usually take "water" here to mean baptism. What he saw when he read the Nicodemus chapter was the profound significance of a new birth as the way of entering into the kingdom. He saw in it a spiritual act and not a ritual one. If the word "born of water" is part of the original text, which many good scholars question, it no doubt means that the writer of it admitted the importance of the ritual act, but it was for him, in any case, wholly inadequate without the vital and transforming inward process, wrought upon the soul by the work of the Spirit. Man is born from above into the spiritual life by the work of the divine Spirit—and there is no substitute for that creative "birth".

The Quaker found in Scripture what he was looking for, as is the case with most readers who are not historically and critically trained—it sometimes happens even with those who are !—and he read over what did not concern him as with eyes that saw not. Here in "John" he lighted upon the truths which formed the substance of his faith and practice. The things which are done to the flesh—to the body—do not avail, fall short of the mark. Religion has to do with *the spirit of the man*, and only when this inner self is reached with a vital force which makes the whole life new has the essential act taken place. The Word of God took on our human nature and lived among us, and loved, and suffered, that we might see how human life can be raised to a divine level by a higher Spirit and how the most perfect love and consecration can be revealed through simple acts of humility and daily service, such as washing the dusty feet of toiling men. It is *that*, and not ritual, which is raised to its full glory in " John's " Gospel. Without anything to " draw with ", and without any actual water from the well, Christ makes the simple Samaritan woman see that he can give her " living water ", can give an inner spring of life which will gather volume and power as the years grow, and will well up to eternal life, so that she will not thirst any more, nor " come hither to draw ". This incident at Jacob's Well follows immediately upon the statement that " Jesus did not Himself baptize with water ". The account proceeds to tell what He does do instead of baptizing with water. He initiates eternal life in the soul. He supplies the water of life which becomes a perennial source of spiritual life, supplanting the old thirsts that make life futile, and quickening all the deeper forces of the interior life. The book of Ecclesiasticus (xxiv. 21) had represented Wisdom as saying : " Those who eat me will always hunger for me again ; those who drink me will always thirst for me." Christ, in the discourse at the well, presents Himself as the spiritual substance which vitalizes the inner man and enables him in his turn to be a source of life to others.

Here, in the Fourth Gospel, then, read with eyes alert for a spiritual religion, the Quakers found the charter of their faith. It was here that they found the great words about spiritual worship which they wore as their frontlet : " God is Spirit and they that worship Him must worship Him in spirit and in truth." Here also they found a form of Christianity which seemed to them to consist essentially of life, of light, of love, of truth and of the Spirit revealed in man. There was more ritualism implied in the narrative than they took note of, but they found what they wanted, namely, a way of life with the whole emphasis on the inner nature, and with every step of it *a vital process*. They came to feel that the only baptism that really mattered was the creative, initiatory work of the Spirit within, bringing the soul up out of its submerged and buried life to a real " birth " into a spiritual kingdom of life—" the water that I shall give you shall be in you as a well of water springing up into eternal life ". And they came to feel that the only essential communion was the experience of partaking through Christ of the Life of God revealed in their souls. They sought to find the reality which could be only *symbolized* in bread and wine, and having found the reality, they dispensed with the symbol.

Some persons feel the need for symbols much more than others do. It turns largely upon the type of imagination which one possesses whether they are needed or not. Some feel hindered in their spiritual life by symbolism, and others can make almost no progress without it. It is impossible in these matters to lay down fixed and general rules. There are patriots who care little or nothing for the help of symbols, such as the flag or the national hymn ; they have their ideal of the country, and for that they live and sacrifice. There are other patriots, however, who are swept by a powerful emotion at the sight of the national colours, or at the sound of the well-known words which glorify the land they love, and they have their deepest affection stirred only through these symbols. It is the same way in the sphere of religion. It seems impossible to many persons to worship without some visible, or tangible, or auditory stimulus—what Robert Browning calls " mid-way helps ". This is a psychological situation, and it would seem to be a mistake to try to have only one type and method of worship for all mankind. The different types need not be ranked as higher or lower. They only need to be recognized as psychologically and characteristically different. There will be good persons, spiritual persons, persons of depth and insight among the symbolizers, and equally so among the non-symbolizers, and there will be some who are at home in both types.

The Friends are, to a large extent, weak in symbolizing power. They do not feel the need of the " mid-way helps ". They are arrested and hindered by the visible and tangible symbols. They want to be left to deal directly and immediately with the great realities by which they live. There are times when they do not want *words*, even though they may be very good words. They want to feel the fresh, free currents of life without any sound or voice. They have a fear of stopping with the outward symbol and of not getting beyond it to that deeper reality for which it stands. The result is that throughout their history, they have preferred to seek for the baptism of the Spirit without the use of water, and to experience a communion of soul with the living Christ without the use of bread and wine.

It will appear odd to some, no doubt, that a small body of Christians, as Friends are, should break with the rest of Christendom in a matter which has always seemed to so many members of the Church a vital and essential feature of religious faith and practice. The historical fact confronts us at once that there have been very great differences in the history of the Church both as to the real meaning of the sacraments and as to the way in which they should be administered in order to be *efficacious*. There is no unanimity of judgment, and there is no arbiter who can pronounce authoritatively for us all. I can hardly do better than quote on this point the words of Bishop Jayne of Chester, England. He wrote in 1919 : " I am bound to point out that we are thwarted in all our attempts to promote the Kingdom by the sad and most mysterious fact that for centuries, in East and West, the Holy Communion has notoriously been the storm-centre of bitter controversy and division throughout Christendom. No truth of Christianity has undergone more strange perversions or has been more grievously deflected and distorted out of shape than the doctrine of the Holy Eucharist. If you wish to know how Christians can hate one another, you have only to read the later history of the Sacrament of our Saviour's dying love. If you wish to know the lowest and grossest depth of superstition within the circle of the Christian Church, you have only to turn to the same history. Truly our Table has become a snare to us ; the marvel is that it has survived its own corruptions."

In the last analysis, each branch of the Christian Church follows the practice which it believes to be nearest to the divine pattern, and each one tests its practice in the light of the spiritual effect which the practice produces upon its members' lives. That is precisely what the Friends do. They sincerely believe that they have found a living way in union and com-

G

munion with God, and they are convinced that it is a way which produces lives of sweetness, fragrance and spiritual power.

In early periods of Quaker history, the opponents of the Friends could and did often criticize their position by insisting that they were neglecting to obey positive commands of Christ and to keep definite ordinances which He Himself instituted. They have always answered that they found no such positive commands, nor any clear evidence that He instituted external ceremonies. There are now, as is well known, sound spiritually minded scholars of almost every communion in Christendom who take this position. Professor Jülicher said in 1898, " Jesus inaugurated nothing, instituted nothing". Professor Spitta, at the same date, wrote : " All thought of an intention to found a rite for the observance of the Church is out of the question." Professor T. R. Glover said, in his *Conflict of Religions* (p. 158) : " There is a growing consensus among independent scholars that Jesus instituted no sacraments, yet Paul found the rudiments of them among the Christians and believed he had the warrant of Jesus for the heightening which he gave them." Dean Hastings Rashdall, in his Bampton Lectures on *The Idea of the Atonement*, says : " The words, ' This do in remembrance of Me ', may certainly be regarded as a later addition. . . . If we set these words aside, there is nothing to suggest that our Lord had the intention of founding an institution or permanent rite of any kind."

Friends arrived at their position by intuition and by their constant use of the Fourth Gospel, rather than by historical and critical research, but the slower and surer methods of study are verifying the soundness of

their insight. Spiritual practices and acts of worship
and communion should not in any case rest upon commands as their basis. It ought to be seen by every
penetrating worshipper that Christianity is not a
religion of commandments and ordinances, but a religion of life and spirit. The real test of a method of
worship is to be found, not in its origin, but in its
function and its power. There is no question that the
apostolic Church had sacraments. They are plainly
in evidence throughout the New Testament period.
They were at first extremely simple and vital. The
little fellowships, which were like " tiny islands in a
vast sea of paganism ", met for a community meal,
which was called the " Agape ", " the eating of bread
in joy and gladness and love ". It was eaten as a
memorial meal and with an exalted sense of Christ's
invisible presence in the group. The fellowship (Koino-
nia) was felt to be more than a human and finite unity ;
it was for them a time of communion in life and spirit
with the living Head of their group felt to be present
there in their midst. The expansion and reorganiza-
tion of this simple community meal took place, first,
in Corinth. The reinterpretation of the Supper is set
forth in that extraordinary passage which is found in
1 Cor. xi. 17–34. From that time on, the Supper
tended to pass from its simple original meaning to a
mysterious and magical event by which the participant
believed that he received " the medicine of immortality
and the antidote of death " (St. Ignatius).

Something quite similar happened in the case of
baptism. It was at first a very simple way of initiation into the life of the fellowship. One marked his
break with his old life and associations by a positive
act of separation and cleansing, symbolized by the

application of water. It was taken at first, as all the New Testament instances indicate, " in the name of Christ ", as a way of entering His fellowship. Its importance could not have been felt to be very great or the accounts of it would have been more specific and detailed. St. Paul's attitude toward it is very casual : " I baptized the household of Stephanas, but no one else, *as far as I remember*. Christ did not send me to baptize, but to preach the gospel " (1 Cor. 1–17). " John " goes out of his way to emphasize the fact that Jesus did to baptize. Its importance, however, increases steadily with the advance of time, even in the New Testament period, and the trinitarian formula is added at the end of Matthew (xxviii. 19), as though it had been used from the first. By Tertullian's time (about 150–225 A.D.), the belief was already current that the baptismal water was changed into divine material and that the application of it actually destroyed the germs of original sin and the sins committed up to that moment. Tertullian calls it " the medicinal bath of regeneration " and he gives this amazing account of its efficacy : " Without pomp, without any novel preparations, and without cost, a man is sent down into the water and baptized, a few words are spoken and he rises out of the water again, little or nothing cleaner, but with his attainment of eternity settled " (de Bap. 4). Whatever one may think of the apostolic origin of these two sacraments, no one with sound historical judgment can suppose that sacraments in the sense implied by the words of St. Ignatius and Tertullian existed when the Church was *new*.

It is after all not so much their failure to appreciate symbols that has carried Friends away from the external use of sacraments as it is their desire to shake themselves entirely free from the implications of *magic*. Magic is a subtle power, and it makes its way into the practices of religion to a far greater extent than most persons are aware. There are phrases in many prayers that are relics of it. There are many sacerdotal practices which unconsciously carry on into our scientific century words and customs that have been borrowed from ancient magic. One sees, in following Luther's fierce controversies over Baptism and the Supper, what a gripping hold upon him the magical features of the sacraments had gained. We sometimes suppose that Protestantism left behind the superstitions and accumulations of magic which so deeply marked mediæval Christianity. But the facts do not quite bear out that easy faith and hope. There is still a long journey to take before these things are left behind.

Friends have made an honest effort to take that last step which the Reformation obviously did not take. They have wished to exhibit a genuinely *spiritual* religion, washed clean of superstition and magic. They have wanted every step and stage of salvation and of worship to be *a living process*. They are afraid of phrases which are supposed to have some *sacred* efficacy. They are anxious not to have officials who belong in a special class and are assumed to have peculiar powers that others lack. They do not recognize places or buildings as having any inherent sanctity. They count only on those operations which are truly ethical and spiritual; that is, those operations which produce in the person *a new spirit and a new power to live by*. The religious life, for them, is witnessed by a new creation. There are no substitutes for life; there is nothing that can take the place of the momentous spiritual event.

Friends do not, however, belittle the reverent and spiritual use of sacraments whenever they see them used in Spirit and in Truth as a part of vital worship. They do not feel the need of them for themselves, but they can usually recognize genuine worship and feel thankful for it though the form may vary from their own type. They are neither propagandists nor iconoclasts. They want the largest freedom to prevail. They desire to have men come to God in the way that seems most real and vital and effective. It is best in these deep and awesome matters to speak with restraint and gentleness, to be tender and eager to catch the inner meaning, to walk softly and impute only the best motives. We do well to remember Tennyson's noble words :

> O thou that after toil and storm
>   Mayst seem to have reach'd a purer air,
>   Whose faith hath centre everywhere,
> Nor cares to fix itself to form,

> Leave thou thy sister when she prays
>   Her early Heaven, her happy views ;
>   Nor thou with shadow'd hint confuse
> A life that leads melodious days.

> Her faith through form is pure as thine,
>   Her hands are quicker unto good :
>   O, sacred be the flesh and blood
> To which she links a truth divine !

> See thou, that countest reason ripe
>   In holding by the law within,
>   Thou fail not in a world of sin,
> And ev'n for want of such a type.

Acts that have drawn transcendent meanings up

> From the best passion of all bygone time,
> Steeped through with tears of triumph and remorse,
> Sweet with all sainthood, cleansed in martyr-fires,

deserve to be treated with a spirit of love and sympathy, not with the methods of the forum and the arena. It is well that we should learn to view all these matters of faith with breadth, with charity, with liberality and with catholicity. But conviction and inward sincerity are also great traits of life. The world will always need those who are ready to go forward on a lonely road, those who care more for what is true than for what is ancient and customary, those who have inward vision and can live by invisible realities. Nothing is more important than the slow, age-long task of building up a spiritual humanity, of leaving the swaddling clothes of childhood for the deeper experiences of the full-grown man.

CHAPTER VI

SIMPLICITY AND DEPTH OF LIFE

WE are all concerned to discover a way to build our civilization on a new and better foundation. We shall be occupied with the problems of that task in later chapters, but it will prove to be a sound conclusion that we must first build rightly the inward life and spirit of the individual person. Society is not the mere mathematical sum of the parts ; no organic unity ever is. But we shall never get a good society until the composing units are good persons. We have here one of those tantalizing circular processes which so often confront us. The type of society which exists at any time is an immense factor in determining the quality of the individual person, and at the same time the quality of the component persons makes the character of the society. It is a puzzle over which we need not waste much of our limited stock of good grey matter. The important business in hand is getting as many good persons as possible and bringing them constructively into vital function, and each one of us can probably be most effective by concentrating upon the inward formation of what we proverbially call " number one ".

The Quakers have always been concerned, as we shall see, about the task of building a better social world, but they have been no less concerned over the formation of a single unit. This seems almost certainly to have been the point of focus in Christ's spiritual mission, and it comes to the front in all great religious endeavours. The *life* of a person is more precious than the gold of Ophir and outweighs in intrinsic worth all the yellow wealth of the world. This is not an article in any of the historical creeds, but it is written in large letters in the fundamental charter of the soul, and Christ set it as a frontlet on every brow. The Quakers in the seventeenth century rediscovered the principle and underscored it, sometimes indeed with their own blood. This intrinsic worth of the individual sprang for them out of the divine possibilities inherent in the soul of man. They did not believe in the divine right of Stuart kings, but they did believe in the divine right of every soul. There is something sublime and august about *the consciousness of ought* which rises above all the noises and confusions of the world. A being that has that *voice* in his inmost shechinah is not just a creature of time and space and matter. He comes out of the Deep and is still inwardly linked with the Deep.

We have seen how the Quaker way of worship is organized to cultivate this deeper and diviner aspect of life. But there are other features of life no less important than worship and occupying a far larger proportion of the day and week. The atmosphere and climate of one's ordinary daily life, the outlook and expectation, the central ambition of the person's real life—those are the things which in the long run largely settle what kind of person one is to be. There are certain mental states which lock up our lives with restraints, fears and inhibitions. There are other states and attitudes which liberate us, release our forces and send us forward conquering and to conquer. Resolves and determined purposes, formed at the centre of the inner life, are mighty energies, and even day-dreams and the subtle mental stuff of our reveries play a more important rôle in the drama of our lives than we usually are aware of. In any case, the persistent habits of thought, the dominant ideal aims, may be counted as the major factors in making a person the type of being that he becomes.

In all the best generations of Quakerism, the ideal aim and the controlling expectation of the wiser members have been to live *the simple life*. It is, of course, a vague and indefinable term. It is not a magic phrase by which one can do just the opposite of the miracle of Aladdin's lamp, and suddenly leap from the extravagance of palatial living to the quiet Eden of a one-roomed cottage, with bark dishes and wooden spoons. The simple life does not begin outside, with the house or the spoons. It begins inside, with *the quality of the soul*. It is first and foremost the quality of sincerity, which is the opposite of duplicity or sham. Emerson's famous line, " Your life talks so loudly that I cannot hear the words you say ", makes the idea pretty clear. The fountain must be right, if we want the water to be clear. Unclouded honesty at the heart and centre of the man is the true basis of simplicity. The tone of a bell is settled by the quality of the constituent metal, and, if that is wrong in stuff and mixture, you will not get a good bell by putting on a coat of fine paint.

This kind of simple life will call, among other things, for an attitude of meekness and humility. But those traits are always consistent with manliness and dignity. The meek person is not a Uriah Heap; the humble person is not a doormat. To be " meek " is to have a true, honest estimate of your life—it is to see yourself as you are, without any artificial inflation. All one needs to do, if he means to be " humble ", is to keep a constant contrast in mind between himself as he now is and that larger, truer, richer potential self which he all the time feels hidden away within himself. Perhaps this is what is meant by " the white stone with a new name written on it, which no man knoweth *save he that hath it* ". It involves not merely honesty and sincerity in all the relationships with one's fellow men, but it calls also for utter clarity of spirit in all one's relationships with God. It is extremely easy to be insincere in prayer, to say words which have no *intention* behind them, to strain for high-sounding phrases which, however, do not carry a freight of real meaning. The highest reach of sincerity is surely to be found in the resolve of soul to maintain an unsullied *honour* before God and to be in His sight what we *seem* to be. That has been persistently, I believe, the honest aspiration of the serious-minded Quaker.

This trait of simplicity has been very clearly in evidence in the Quaker aversion to creeds and formulations of doctrine. The Friends have not been rebels in their attitude toward the great central truths of Christendom. They have usually preserved a profound evangelical spirit and devotion. But they did not want to have their lives or their faith complicated by the wholesale adoption of words and phrases coined in other centuries, coloured by the battle-temper of ancient issues and incapable to-day of the same meaning which they originally bore to their formulators. They find it difficult to be absolutely honest and sun-clear when they undertake to use these inherited statements of bygone ages. Such phrases do not truly interpret the heart's deepest meanings. They engender controversy and strife. Instead of unifying Christendom, they divide it. Instead of forming into one irresistible array the spiritual forces of the world, they tend to form groups of contending partisans—opposing each other instead of turning to conquer the evil and darkness of the world. But the essential difficulty is the inner difficulty of maintaining one's moral honesty and sincerity. The words by which we express our deepest faith must be not only rich with the experience of the saints and martyrs of the past, but they must also interpret for us the living, present truth of our time ; they must be consistent with all *we* have proved and verified, and they must be tested by our own soul's experience. The Quaker means this by his aim at simplicity. Few things are more needed to-day than this plain, simple note that religion, on its upward-reaching side, is just joyous companionship with God—with God who is nearer than Abraham realized when he talked with Him at his tent door, or Jacob dreamed when he saw Heaven at the far end of a ladder.

But I pass from simplicity in the inner life and in worship to the " simple life " in the narrower sense. We come now to problems of business, of dress, of recreation, of entertainment, of culture, of luxury, in short to the world-old problem of how to live a Christian life, not in a cloister or an anchorite's cave, but in an eager, busy, complex world of more or less imperfect men and women. The saint of an earlier day tried to cut the knot by withdrawal. He climbed a lonely pillar, or he buried himself in a quiet cell, but even so he could not escape the self which he carried with him. All his problems came back in new fashion, and as far as he succeeded in cutting the bonds which bound him to his fellows he found himself shrinking and shrivelling like a severed branch.

The endeavour to win goodness by withdrawal from society is as vain as the search for the lost fountain or the pursuit of an alchemy which will make gold out of lead. The only possible way to overcome the world is to carry the forces of the spiritual life into the veins of society until peace and love and righteousness prevail there.

We can best discover the principle of the simple life by a contrast with the spirit of commercialism. The commercial spirit is selfish. Its motto is " Expand to get ". Even its philanthropies are selfish. They are to whitewash gigantic schemes of absorption. Its culture is selfish. It is veneer and display. The trail of selfishness is on its art and music and religion and recreation. In the interest of selfish pleasure it would turn the automobile into a juggernaut and take little boys out of places of spiritual influence to make caddies for Sunday golf. It is the old Pagan Roman spirit modernized and sprinkled with a little baptismal water, but essentially the spirit of selfishness—the pursuit of power, pleasure and luxury for their own sake. Over against it, at its antipodes, is the spirit of the simple life. It can be lived at any level of poverty or wealth ; and at any stage of ignorance or culture. It is essentially the spirit of *living for life's sake*, or consecration to personal and social goodness. Its first aim is making a life rather than making a living. This spirit does not keep a man out of commercial business, nor does it command him to confine his business to narrow limits and to small returns. But if he is to belong to the goodly fellowship of those who live the simple life, his business must be made an avenue of ministering to human life. It must be to him what the mission field is to the missionary—a sphere for manifesting his consecration to service. " If I were not a priest ", says Tauler, an apostle of the simple life in the fourteenth century, " I should esteem it a gift of the Holy Ghost that I was able to make shoes." And we may add that the latter occupation may be turned to divine service as well as the other. I know a Friend who has served God through his business as much as though he had been ordained bishop of his diocese. His spirit has remained simple and childlike as his business has expanded, and he has made the wheels of his factory turn to man's service. I might just as well have chosen my illustration from the life of a farmer whom I know, who tills his cabbage patch and corn field to the glory of God and the service of man. His acres are broad, his days are crowded, but his home is a home of the simple life.

The same principle applies to *culture*. There are no limits to the pursuit of culture so long as it is sought in the spirit of consecration and for ends of service. Like the Master, who fully embodied the idea of the simple life, we can say, " For their sakes I enlarge and cultivate myself, that others may also enter a more abundant life ". The test of any of the culture-fields is whether it can be made a means of personal enlargement and of wider consecration. Poetry, art and music belong to the simple life, if they minister to man's larger life, and if they do not belong there they do not so minister. The question is not one of theory, but one of practice. Beauty is as genuine a reality as truth is, and so is harmony. Pursued in the aim of enlargement and for widening the area of life and happiness, they are as legitimate, and as " simple ",

as the reading of *Pilgrim's Progress* or *Piety Promoted*.
Doubtless they may be turned to low ends, but so, too,
may all other earthly pursuits. The easy solution is
to hedge life about with " thou shalt nots ", to draw
a narrow circle and to limit life to beaten paths of
commonplace virtue. But that produces mediocre lives.
It squeezes life down to a level of sameness. It
endangers advance and risks the extinction of origin-
ality, freshness and power. Simplicity is not barren-
ness. It is singleness of aim and purpose. There are
few more splendid illustrations of the simple life of
culture than Michael Angelo. He rounded St. Peter's
dome and hung it in air. He painted the immortal
frescoes on the ceiling of the Sistine Chapel. He
carved that most majestic figure of the lawgiver Moses,
and that eternally youthful face of David, the shepherd
king and psalmist. He wrote sonnets, which by themselves would have given him a permanent place among
great creators. And yet this man writes to his father :
" It is enough to have bread, and to live in the faith
of Christ, as I do here, for I live humbly ; neither do
I care for the life or honours of the world ". He turned
every conquest to spiritual ends. He mastered difficult
tasks and won skill in many fields, only that he might
be a greater spiritual force and make his life count
more in the slow work of producing a world full of truth
and goodness and beauty.

The principle has, in most perfect words, been
expressed by John Woolman : " To turn all we possess
into the channel of universal love becomes the business
of our lives." That is the Quaker message about the
simple life. The pillar Friends have always preached
enlargement of life, but they have, at the same time,
guarded the simplicity of life by pulsing a single pur-

pose through all their pursuits, and by baptizing their culture with the dew of consecration. On this principle there are no dangers. The full life may be as simple as the barren life; the life which brings in spoil from every field of culture may possess the simple directness of a line of light.

Little need be said about simplicity of speech. A person of genuine sincerity and of single purpose—a person who has cut loose for ever from sham and duplicity—will say what he means in good plain language. He will have no use for an oath, for all that he speaks will be upon honour and in the fear of God, and he will make his " yea " on any occasion weigh as heavy as a Bible oath. But he will go farther. He will halt at the brave simplicity of actual facts, and he will shun exaggeration and superlative phrases as he would shun the enforcement of truth by an oath. The simple truth is always mighty, and needs no fire-crackers or cannon.

Ever since the fig-leaf aprons of Eden, dress has been a bothersome problem. It is one of those things which very easily get to be an end in themselves, and it may even, as it often has done, outweigh in importance the development of the personal life itself. In the days of Elizabeth it is said that " the dressing of a fine lady was more complicated than the rigging of a ship ". The persistent aim of Quaker simplicity is to put dress in proper subordination to life itself. Here again no artificial system will accomplish the true end. It is a personal problem. Dress is a somewhat sacred matter. It is everybody's right, and, I believe, duty to look well, to have a becoming appearance. A person is actually more of a person well dressed than slovenly dressed. But attention must not centre on the clothes.

They are for the person, not he for them.   That person
is most suitably dressed whose life makes so much of
an impression that his clothes are not thought about,
and who stimulates a desire to imitate his character,
rather than an ambition to rival his expensive garb.
William Penn's maxim is a sound one : " Excess in
apparel is a costly folly.   The very trimming of the
vain world would clothe the naked.   If thou art clean
and warm it is sufficient ; for more doth but rob the
poor.   It is said of the true Church, ' the king's daughter
is all glorious within '.   Let our care, therefore, be of our
minds more than of our bodies, if we would be of her
communion."   Furthermore, as John Woolman has
forcefully pointed out, " every degree of luxury hath
connection with unnecessary labour ", and therefore
simplicity in personal attire has a far-reaching social
import.

I shall touch but one more aspect of this principle of
simplicity—simplicity in recreation.   Play is a fundamental need of personal life, and the person who does
not know how to do it wisely and well always suffers
for it.   The exercise of physical powers, the joy of
activity, are instructive.   The baby kicks, just to get
the kick, not because it has a further end in view.   The
athletic spirit is grounded in the actual needs of youthful life.   The stress and strain of labour and responsibility in later life demand relaxation, and every quality
of work and service is heightened by proper recreation.
Life is worth more from every point of view if it has a
bloom of joy and freshness upon it, and if the nerves
get suitable chances to shake out their tension.

But here again our principle applies.   Life is not for
play and recreation.   They are for life.   The man of
the simple life makes his recreations minister to the

H

true fulfilment of his being. He will not allow them to swallow him up. Even in his lighter pursuits he is still captain of his soul, and he counts only those things lawful and expedient which make for his own enlargement, and which cast no shadow of evil upon the lives of his fellows. This is, I believe, the spirit, though it may not always have been the practice of Quaker simplicity. The London Book of Discipline wisely says : "The life of the Christian is not a dull and cheerless existence." It is not for the diminution but for the increase of happiness that all occupations are to be "baptized into the Christian spirit". It is the very heart and fibre of the Quaker faith that this brief earthly span is our chance at the prize of learning how to live. Its real emphasis then is on the preciousness of life itself.

One of the most serious weaknesses in the entire period of Quaker history has been the mistaken attempt to get simplicity by easy, short-cut methods. Friends have again and again endeavoured to maintain a poor, artificial form of simplicity by "regulating" speech, and manner and garb. In the long middle-age period of their history, they glorified the use of " thee " and "thou", as though this form of " plain speech ", as they called it, had some saving efficiency. They tried to explain it and defend it as " Scriptural language ". They even claimed that it was to be the language of heaven, as it was obviously the mode of speech used when the Almighty was addressed. But all the time, it really stood in the mind of the Quaker as a badge of peculiarity. He had in his middle period surrendered his early faith that the principle of the inward light was to conquer the world and that the Society of Friends was to be the beginning of the true Church

Universal. He had settled back to the lower ideal that in the midst of the wayward world and the imperfect forms of Christianity, the little band of Quakers were " a chosen and peculiar people "—" a saving remnant of the true Israel of God ". That was, of course, a good deal of a " drop " from the primitive expectation, and as the shrunk, cooled and soberer ideal came to prevail, the aspiration for genuine simplicity was translated into a fixed type of plainness and simplicity. To say " you " to a single person was to belong to the great world of fashion. To say " thou " was to announce oneself as " peculiar " and as a member of a " plain people ", separated from the vain and contaminating world. The same importance attached to the use of numerical names for the days of the week and for the months. The popular names were said to be derived from " heathen gods and goddesses ". With scrupulous care the Quaker said " First day " and never " Sunday " ; he said " Fifth month " and never " May ". This, again, was assumed to be " plainness and simplicity ", though it was really the badge and sign of " a peculiar people ".

Even greater stress was laid on the " plainness of apparel ". That did not, however, mean the choice of a simple, quiet type of dress, sober and inexpensive ; it meant rather a set and approved form of dress. It amounted practically to the ritual of a garb. Once more the idea of " peculiarity " was the prominent thing and the dress or the hat was the badge and sign. The " plain " garb was advocated and urged as a " hedge and defence " against manners and customs of the world. It was pointed out that one who wore the " peculiar dress " would thereby escape the solicitations of the evil world and would remove from himself the temptations to enter places of amusement where his garb would make him look odd.

It was no doubt a " hedge ", but, after all, it was a poor expedient. For a weak and timid soul, an external hedge like that may have offered a refuge and a way of safety. But the only true defence in this world of temptation is *a rightly fashioned will,* a spirit that has learned to choose and discriminate and that *prefers* the pure and the good. It is a mark of moral weakness to need to wear " a garb of defence ", it appears to indicate that the inward fibre is not yet formed and that the soul is not " crowned and mitred ". It was a mistaken course from which the Society of Friends at large has recovered. It reduced simplicity to a rule, it indicated a drop to the status of a " peculiar people ", it stressed an outward instead of an inward protection from the evil of the world, and it tended to turn a religion of joy and faith into a drab system of rules and restraints. It raised " discipline " to far too great a prominence and it focused attention upon an outward instead of upon the really important matter of an inward experience and power. It played a good deal of havoc with those great first ideals, but it did produce, notwithstanding, a beautiful piety and it assisted the culture of a sweet and fragrant saintliness. The great problem, now that the hedge is gone and the ideal of being a peculiar people has passed, is to maintain a true simplicity, to produce a genuine inborn piety and to form saints who wear the white samite of a pure and virile inward spirit.

Simplicity does not mean shallowness. It is not the same thing as superficiality. A life can be very simple without being either thin or narrow. Some of the simplest of Christ's sayings have a bottomless depth to them. And I think that it can be honestly said that the Quakers have harmoniously united simplicity of life with depth of life. One of Brother Lawrence's companions said of him that he had " a spaciousness of mind quite beyond the range of the ordinary poor lay-brother, a penetration that surpassed all expectation ". Here was a man who was utterly simple and naïve and who did the most common menial tasks with his hands, but his fellow companions were struck with the spaciousness of his mind. I have often noticed the most unusual dimensions of life in quiet, simple Friends. They often seem to have qualities of grace, culture and breeding, even when they have always lived in a rural district, far remote from the visible sources of culture and refinement. Sagacity, largeness of view, wisdom in counsel, magnanimity of spirit fit in perfectly with Quaker simplicity. There are, of course, too many Quakers who have neither simplicity nor spaciousness, but where the former quality is attained the latter one is apt to be present.

John Woolman is one of the finest specimens of these rare and beautiful qualities. His saintliness was transparent in its simplicity, his walk with God was tremblingly humble, but he had a depth of wisdom and a vision of penetration that reached to the bottom of a problem or an issue and laid hold upon an eternal principle of truth and righteousness. Joseph Sturge was a similar spirit in a later age,

> The crystal clearness of an eye kept single
> Shamed all the frauds of man.

> A fine sense of right
> And Truth's directness, meeting each occasion
> Straight as a line of light.

John G. Whittier, who wrote these lines on Joseph Sturge, had the same combination of qualities himself. They have appeared in many public Friends whose ministry had power and convicting force, not from its freight of ideas, but from its depth of experience and its calm note of reality. But even more impressive is the large array of ordinary, unnamed Friends who had no fame and no publicity, but who were saints in the farm-house and leaders of light and truth in their communities, by the sheer strength of their inward life and by the simplicity and spaciousness of their souls.

CHAPTER VII

THE QUAKERS AS PEACE-MAKERS

IT is a mistake to call Quakers " non-resisters " or " passivists ". They are neither. They do not face any giant evil with a passive attitude. They seek always to organize and to level against it the most effective forces there are. They know as well as anybody does that instincts and passions are not changed by miracle and that peace cannot prevail where injustice and hate are rampant. They seek to do away with war by first doing away with the causes and occasions for it ; that is, by removing the fundamental grounds from which war springs, by eliminating the roots and seeds of it in the social order, and by forming an atmosphere and climate that make war unthinkable. This means, of course, that peace-making is " big business ".

The forerunners of the Quakers had for some centuries before George Fox been opposed to war. The Waldenses were strict and scrupulous in their refusal to fight or to take life in any way. Many of the small heretical sects before the Reformation had similar views on these matters. The Anabaptists were divided in their conclusions about the right of a Christian to bear a sword and they varied in their practice, though there was a large wing of the movement that refused utterly to have any part in war. The influence of Erasmus, the greatest of the humanists, upon the scattered groups of spiritual reformers was very profound. He discounted the value of dogma and theology and turned instead with freshly awakened interest to the original teachings of Jesus. Every page of the New Testament, he declared, " speaks of little else but peace and concord ; and yet the whole life of the greater portion of Christians is employed in nothing so much as the concerns of war. . . . It were best to lay aside the name of Christian at once, or else to give proof of the teaching of Christ by its only criterion, brotherly love ". It was no doubt the rediscovery of the message of the New Testament that swung Erasmus so strongly against the spirit and methods of war. This note of opposition to war, which receives its most powerful expression in the great scholar's *Querola pacis*, from which I have quoted above, recurs again and again in his writings. He was one of the major shaping influences in the life and thought of the spiritual reformers. They held his view of the freedom of the will ; they shared his revolt from theology ; they returned with him to the primitive teaching of Jesus, and they felt as he did about the prevailing evils of society and about the wickedness of war. Gentleness, love, grace, light, truth and the forces of the Spirit are their armoury. They had no fixed propaganda. They quietly and simply taught a way of life with which war was entirely incompatible. " What will Christ say ", Jacob Boehme asks the ministers of his day, " when He sees your apostolic hearts covered with armour ? When He gave you the sword of the Spirit, did He command you to fight and make war, to put on the sword and kill ? "

George Fox gives us no clue by which we can trace

the origin and development of his own position toward war. His outlook and attitude are in every particular similar to the outlook and attitude of these predecessors, but he never quotes them and he supplies no positive evidence of direct correspondence with them. The influences which shaped his mind in this direction were almost certainly subconscious influences, though his constant absorption with the New Testament was without question one of the leading forces that set his thought into antagonism with war. His earliest positive reaction is the famous response which Fox made while in Derby jail to the Commissioners who proposed to make him the captain of a troop of soldiers in the Commonwealth Army. " I told them ", he says, " that I lived in the virtue of that life and power that takes away the occasion of all wars." . . . " I was come into the covenant of peace which was before wars and strifes were." It was a remarkable position for a young man to take and it was oddly enough expressed. The " covenant of peace " into which he had come was almost certainly in his mind the life of the Spirit. He felt that he was raised to the nature and type of the new Adam and was forever done with the ways of the Adam who fell, and it seemed to him that the new and higher life entailed a spirit and method of life which were essentially Christlike. It is a way of life that practises love and forbearance. It seeks to give rather than to get. It conquers by grace and gentleness. It prefers to suffer injustice than in the slightest degree to do it. It wins and triumphs by sacrifice and self-giving. It spreads abroad an atmosphere of trust and confidence and proposes to prepare the way for a new world by creation of a new spirit—which is essentially the spirit of the Cross. If every one

lived thus, there would be " no occasion of war " but
" a covenant of peace ".

That is the birth of the Quaker " testimony " for
peace. Fox laid down no rules for his followers. He
formulated no prohibitions. He was easy and lenient
toward those who were in the army or the navy and
who nevertheless wanted to become " Children of the
Light ". He always left them free to " follow their
light ". He seems to have felt sure that their inward
guidance would eventually bring them to " the covenant of peace " which he had found in his own way.
There is an interesting tradition that William Penn
asked George Fox whether it was right for him to continue his custom of wearing his sword, and that Fox
answered, " Wear it as long as thou canst " ; i.e. wear
it until conscience makes it clear that a sword is not
consistent with Christian life and profession. The
early Friends in Fox's lifetime did extremely little to
clarify and interpret their position any further in this
matter. Fox himself frequently uses the phrase,
" Our weapons are spiritual, not carnal ". That may
be taken, I think, as the substance of the Quaker
position in the first generation. They were not absolute
" non-resisters ", but they put their faith and confidence
in the gentler forces of the Spirit. On one occasion,
when a man rushed at him with a naked rapier, threat-
ening his life, Fox looked at him unmoved and calmly
said, " Alack, poor creature, what wouldst thou do
with thy carnal weapon ? I care no more for it than
I would for a straw ". There was a certain power in
his undisturbed face, a conquering quality in his manner
which enabled him to meet rage, brutality and cruelty
and triumph over them. When the Cambridge
" scholars " tried to pull him off his horse in their

rough, rude sport, he says, " I rid through them in the Lord's power and they cried, ' he shines, he glistens ! ' " An address of Philadelphia Yearly Meeting in 1774 very well expresses the ground and attitude of Friends in this first stage. " Through the influence of the love of Christ in their minds ", it says, " they ceased from conferring with flesh and blood and became obedient to the heavenly vision, in which they clearly saw that all wars and fightings proceeded from the spirit of this world which is at enmity with God, and that they must manifest themselves to be the followers of the Prince of Peace by meekness, humility and patient suffering."

The greatest single event of the early period in the line of peace was the launching of the " Holy Experiment " in Pennsylvania by William Penn. " For the matters of liberty and privilege ", Penn wrote to a friend, " I purpose that which is extraordinary, and leave myself and succession no power of doing mischief, that the will of one man may not hinder the good of a whole country." He guaranteed absolute freedom of conscience, declared that governments exist for the people, laid down the principle that the aim in judicial punishment should be the reformation of the criminal, and he did everything in his power to build a great colony on the foundations of truth, justice, honour, righteousness and peace. Ideals are seldom realized in their full glory of conception and there are flaws in the execution of this noble design, but the Holy Experiment, nevertheless, marks an epoch. Penn also contributed a famous essay toward a peaceable solution of the distracted state of Europe near the end of the seventeenth century. It was called " An essay toward the Present and Future Peace of Europe, by the

Establishment of an European Dyet, Parliament, or Estates ". An incident occurred in Penn's Colony almost a hundred years after it was founded which shows very well how the peace spirit works. In a little settlement on one of the branches of the Monongahela River in Western Pennsylvania shortly before the Revolutionary War, there was a tiny group of Quakers who had migrated from Virginia. Among them was a Friend named Henry Beeson who lived with his family in a cabin in the woods. The Indians were fiercely hostile to the settlers, as these Indians were in sympathetic alliance with the French. A group of Indians surged about the cabin in the night and the family seemed to be doomed unless a miracle occurred. They overheard an old Chief explaining to the Indians that this family belonged to " the broad brims ", who were " William Penn's people ", and that they must not be molested. The Indians quickly withdrew without doing any harm. It was a fine instance of the ancient " miracle " that love and kindness beget love and kindness, even in the hearts of so-called savage men.

Throughout the eighteenth century—a century replete with wars and fightings—Friends were finding their position and slowly defining their attitude. They were also discovering what it costs in blood and suffering to break with the settled habits of centuries and to stand out against the organized and basic requirements of strong, proud nations. Not in great matters were they tested, but in small matters, such as decorating houses and illuminating on occasions of victory, they were called upon to show their mettle. In a paper of " Tender Advice and Caution " drawn up by the Meeting for Sufferings and the London Morning Meeting in 1760, Friends were advised that they should not only " cease from outward hostility, but that their conversation and conduct must be consistent and *of a piece throughout*. As they should not join with others in shedding the blood of their fellow creatures, neither could they be one with them in rejoicing for the advantages obtained by such bloodshed ; as they could not fight with the fighters, neither could they triumph with the conquerors ; and therefore they were not to be prevailed upon to make a show of conformity by placing lights in any part of the fronts of their houses ; but patiently suffer whatever violences or abuses were committed against them, for the sake of their peaceable *Christian* Testimony ".

In 1758 the testimony to peace was put before the entire membership of London Yearly Meeting by a special Query to be read and answered by all the Monthly and Quarterly Meetings and by the Yearly Meeting. It asked this positive question : " Do you bear a faithful testimony against bearing arms or paying Trophy Money, or being any way concerned in privateers, letters of marque, or dealing in prize goods ? " In spite of all the efforts of the " concerned and seasoned " Friends, there were always some, and occasionally many, who were easy and inconsistent. The consequences of rigorous fidelity to the peace ideal were usually very hard to bear and it is not surprising that in some instances "·the flesh was weak ". But, with very slight exceptions, the official acts of the Society and the conduct of its spiritualized and representative members were in line with the ideals of peace. One of the severest tests which came to Friends in the eighteenth century was experienced during the Irish Rebellion of 1798, and the test was met in heroic fashion. The brave confidence in higher forces which

these Friends showed when they were face to face with
situations from which no peaceful way of escape seemed
possible, did much to rally the Quaker membership
throughout the world to a renewed fidelity to the war
of peace.

Anthony Benezet of Philadelphia, in a beautiful
treatise published in 1800, put the Quaker position in
admirable form as follows: " There is a remnant who
remain unshakenly convinced that the voice of reason,
the feelings of humanity, and more especially the
gospel of Jesus Christ, call upon them to bear a uniform
testimony against *everything which is inconsistent with
that patience and love which the gospel proposes.* . . .
They can in no wise support that spirit which gives
life to war in any of its branches, but apprehend themselves uniformly called to *promote, to the utmost of their
power, the welfare of all men* " (italics mine).

In this spirit, and with even deeper and tenderer
spirit, John Woolman had called Friends all over the
American Colonies to a way of life consistent with love
and brotherhood. He put the finger of a prophet on
the seat of the trouble when he said that selfishness and
greed lay at the root, not only of slavery, but also of
war. His " Word of Remembrance to the Rich " con-
tains not only child-like wisdom but also sound economic judgment. " When the Spirit of this world which
loves riches ", he says in this remarkable tract, " and
in its working gathers wealth and cleaves to customs
which have their root in self-pleasing, whatever name it
hath, it still desires to defend the treasures it hath
gotten. This is like a chain in which the end of one
link encloseth the end of another. The rising up
of a desire to obtain wealth is the beginning;
this desire being cherished, moves to action; and

riches thus gotten please self ; and while self has a life in them it desires to have them defended. Wealth is attended with power, by which bargains and proceedings contrary to universal righteousness are supported ; and hence oppression carried on with worldly policy and order clothes itself with the name of justice and becomes like a seed of discord in the soul. And as the spirit which wanders from the pure habitation prevails, so the seeds of war swell and sprout and grow and become strong until much fruit is ripened. Then cometh the harvest spoken of by the prophet which is ' an heap in the day of grief and desperate sorrows '. Oh that we may declare against wars and acknowledge our trust to be in God only, may we walk in the light, and therein examine our foundation and motives in holding great estates ! May we look upon our treasures, the furniture of our houses, and our garments, and try whether the seeds of war have nourishment in these our possessions." We only need to add to those great words of an inspired prophet these other words of his which indicate that he was also a consistent saint : " To labour for a perfect redemption from this spirit of oppression is the great business of the whole family of Jesus Christ in this world." In another passage written in the same spirit, Woolman reaches the apex of his triumphant peace position : " It requires ", he says, " much self-denial and resignation of ourselves to God to attain that state wherein we can freely cease from fighting when wrongfully invaded, if, by our fighting there were a probability of overcoming the Invaders. Whoever rightly attains to it, does in some degree feel that Spirit in which our Redeemer gave His life for us."

The nineteenth century gave Friends plenty of

opportunity to test their faith. The Napoleonic wars, the Crimean War, the American Civil War, to mention no others, compelled Friends to search over again their principles of life and to see whether it was possible to live in a society in which armies of offence and defence are an inherent part, and still maintain their peaceable way of life. The English and American Governments for the most part treated Friends very leniently in the several crises. The greatest roll of sufferers was found in the Southern Confederacy during the American Civil War. Friends in this region had two motives for their unvarying refusal to fight. They were, of course, opposed to war *per se* and they were determined not to do anything that would fix and maintain slavery as a permanent institution in the States where they lived. The story of their loyalty to conviction is a stirring one and has been well told in F. G. Cartland's *Southern Heroes*.

The great interpretations of the Quaker position in this century were given by Jonathan Dymond in his *Enquiry into the Accordancy of War with the Principles of Christianity* and in his *Essay on War*, by John Bright in his speeches during the Crimean War, and in the poems of John G. Whittier. Friends drew up many official documents and issued many advices, but there was little added in them to make the ideal stand out in any fuller light. There was, on the other hand, a tendency to treat peace as a settled " testimony " of the Society and to deal with it in a dull, lifeless and formal way. Few Friends felt the need of sounding the principle to its basis and bottom and to think it through in all its connections with life and business and in its relations to the existing type of civilization. What they did do in the main was to preserve in the world a body of people who persisted in holding, by word and deed, and through suffering, to the one clear note that was consistent with the way of life which Jesus Christ inaugurated.

But a still more important positive note began to emerge by the middle of the nineteenth century, a note which has not died out and please God never will die out in the hearts of the Quakers. They began to see that it was not enough to stand out for the personal privilege of renouncing war and of living a peaceful life as an individual. They passed over from the mere claim of a privilege to the sense of a weighty obligation. They awoke to the discovery that no man can either live or die unto himself. They came to realize how closely tied into the social fabric we all are. Our noble word obligation means just that. Taken out of Latin and turned over into English it becomes " tied-in-ness ". Anyone who is intending to claim his own right to walk the path of peace must take also his share of the heavy burden of trying to build a world in which the gentler forces of kindness, love, sympathy and co-operation are put into function.

John Woolman had seen that " the seeds of war have nourishment " in the daily lives of men in so far as they encourage luxury and unnecessary worldliness. The spirit of love, therefore, if it is to be effective, must operate not only in war-time, but in those important peace-stretches between wars as well. In short, those who propose to hold aloof from fighting and claim the privileges of peace must become devoted *peace-makers*. This is not to be construed to apply alone to those who bring wars to an end, to diplomats and treaty-makers, nor does it mean in any exclusive sense those who make public peace addresses or who sign petitions or

I

who " post o'er land and ocean without rest " to attend peace conferences and conventions. It applies rather to a deeper and more continuous service of living an everyday life which is "in the covenant of peace ". It means a home-life which exhibits the sway and dominion of love practised in the domain of the family life. It means a neighbourhood life which makes love prevail between man and man, and between woman and woman. It means a business life which translates and interprets, as much at least as one individual can do it, the principles which underlie the sway and kingdom of God. The Friend had tended to live apart. He went his own way, maintained his standing as one of a " peculiar people ", worshipped in isolation from the rest of the community and showed little readiness to share with others his life, his experience or his ideals. If society was "in a mess " it was not his fault. If men stupidly went to war and wasted their substance and had their heads blown off, it was something for which he was not responsible. Gradually, however, this deeper sense of corporate life and responsibility began to dawn upon the more sensitive of the Quakers. A new spirit was born. Other things came to seem more important than hat-brims and bonnets, the problems of garb and speech, the height of grave-stones, and the *patois* of this little Zion. They came out of their quietism and their petty concerns to face the issues of the larger world. They awoke to their responsibilities as citizens, as heads of business, as Christian men. They became magistrates, they stood for Parliament, they went to work to make their operatives comfortable and happy. They did the work of peace-makers in a multitude of ways which were much more important than holding peace meetings.

They widened out their vision and began to think in international terms.

Joseph Sturge and John Bright in England led the way, and in America John G. Whittier was a pioneer of the new idea with many Friends of lesser fame following close behind him. It was an epoch-making step when Joseph Sturge, Henry Pease and Robert Charleton, backed by the London Meeting for Sufferings, went to St. Petersburg to use their influence with the Czar of Russia to prevent the Crimean War, followed a little later by the Quaker mission of love to the war-sufferers on the coasts of Finland, which had been wrecked and made desolate by the British fleet. This was a new way of sharing responsibilities in wartime. A fund of £9,000 ($45,000) was raised for this work of relief. Clothes, food, provision for shelter, fishing-nets, seed-corn for a new harvest, and other necessities of life were supplied to the sufferers around the Gulf of Bothnia, and not only were their lives saved and their means of livelihood reorganized, but their embittered hearts were touched and softened. When three years later the fishermen and peasants of Finland heard of Joseph Sturge's death, their faces were wet with tears and their homes were full of mourning. During the American Civil War, which came a few years later, it was very difficult for Friends to do much constructive work while the war lasted, though they were already organized to care for the hosts of freedmen whom the war liberated. But as soon as the Peace of Appomatox was signed and way opened for it, a noble Quaker from Baltimore, Francis T. King, went effectively to work to provide means for helping to reorganize education in North Carolina and to assist in rebuilding what the war had destroyed.

During the Franco-Prussian War in 1870-1, and after the terrible siege of Paris and the devastating work of the Commune, a band of English Friends went about in the midst of the catastrophe relieving suffering, saving life, reorganizing life, restoring confidence, interpreting in practical and constructive ways and showing to war-victims the deeper rebuilding forces of the spirit. The sum of £200,000 ($1,000,000) was raised for this mission of love, but the spiritual effect was far greater than can be expressed in economic or financial terms.

This service of love amid the horrors and devastations of war prepared the way for the vastly greater work of relief during the years of the Great War and its aftermath. English Friends began even in September 1914 to plan for some way to help the agonized sufferers in the war zones. In the early period of activity, the work of relief had its centre in the Marne district, which had been swept by the merciless storm of modern war. A maternity hospital was established at Châlons-sur-Marne, a children's hospital was opened at Bettancourt and a general hospital at Sermaize, with a convalescent home for tubercular patients at Samöens, in Haute-Savoie. Besides these types of relief, an extensive work of house-building and house-repairing and various forms of agricultural work were carried on through the villages of the Marne valley. As soon as war was declared by the United States, American Friends made arrangements to join with English Friends in this work in the war zones, and large groups of young Friends were trained and sent over to enlarge the amount and the scope of the relief. The call for funds was met with enthusiasm by Friends and others and large sums were raised. As many as six hundred American Friends and others of like ideals joined in the labour of love. Mills were established in the Jura for sawing lumber and building portable houses, and many villages were rebuilt. The hospitals were expanded and equipped and a very large and varied service rendered where it was desperately needed.

After the Armistice was signed and the hope of a new world began to dawn, the political authorities in the district lying between Verdun and Ste. Menehould, including the villages of the Argonne Forest, asked the Quakers to reconstruct that area which had been almost annihilated by the catastrophes of the war. This call was answered favourably, and during the year 1919 the work of rebuilding and reorganizing this area went forward at the hands of a large band of English and American workers. American Friends bought the five extensive army dumps in this part of France and, with the help of two hundred German prisoners and the use of the French railroads, sold them and distributed them to the peasants. The profits were used to build and equip a permanent maternity hospital at Châlons-sur-Marne. One of the villages which these Verdun workers built was named by the villagers *Cité des Amis*.

The thing that counted most through these years of service was the spirit of love and friendship which the workers infused into the hearts and lives of the broken and discouraged peasants among whom they worked. It was a novel experience to have those who felt they could not join in fighting come among them and suffer with them, and at the time of danger and death, repair as far as could be done at the time the havoc and damage of war. It was a new kind of peace-making.

As soon as it was possible to do so, Quaker relief

units set to work in Vienna, in Poland and in Serbia. Two of the French workers went across to Germany and visited all the homes from which the prisoners had come who helped in the Verdun area. These two workers took back to the German homes photographs of the prisoners and paid their families full wages for the period through which the prisoners had worked. Following this, a small group of English and American Friends started relief work in Germany, and in November of 1919 Herbert Hoover asked the American Friends' Service Committee to undertake the immense task of feeding the diseased and undernourished children of Germany. It involved raising large funds and organizing an extensive system of food-distribution, but the work was successfully carried through a term of three years. At the periods of greatest need, as many as one million children were fed daily. The American public responded generously to the call for help and the Friends themselves financed all the costs of maintenance and distribution.

This work proved to be a remarkable service of peace-making. The Germans gradually discovered that their helpers had no selfish ends to serve, that they had come in the spirit of love, to save little children, to promote friendship and fellowship and to help rebuild the new and better world. As this situation dawned upon their minds, they met the proffered kindness with a responding love and friendship, and bonds of peace and fellowship were woven which will not soon be broken. The warm hearts of the Austrians were touched in a similar way by the help and comfort which came to them in their darkest hour. The work of saving the children who had tuberculosis or were threatened with it has been going on in Vienna until the present time. In Russia, too, through revolutions and famine and typhus and malaria, bands of Quaker workers have carried forward a great many forms of saving and relieving service and a spirit of love and reconciliation has been spread widely abroad through this work. Friends have thus endeavoured to be " courageous in the cause of love and in the hate of hate ". They have tried to interpret their message of peace not with words, which soon die and are forgotten, but in deeds which are as immortal as human hearts are. Never again, I think it can be said, will Friends claim the rights and privileges of peace or exemption from the demands of war without making their own contribution to restore the zones of devastation, to bind up the broken-hearted and to show emphatically that spirit which removes the occasion for war. If Friends are to challenge the whole world and claim the right to continue in the ways of peace while everybody else is fighting, they must surely reveal the fact, as they have been endeavouring to do, that they are worthy of peace and that they bear in their body the marks of the Lord Jesus.

Besides the work of construction and relief in war-stricken countries, the English Friends organized a voluntary ambulance unit for non-military service. It began with forty-three men and ended with over six hundred. Twenty of these men gave their lives and many were wounded while engaged in their work for the relief of suffering and distress.

" The Emergency Committee for the Assistance of Germans, Austrians, Hungarians and Turks in Distress", organized by the Meeting for Sufferings in 1914, rendered an immense service to aliens who were stranded in Great Britain. Its work was often of a sort that was unpopular. Its first chairman, Stephen Hobhouse, and several others, were imprisoned for following the line of their duty. It was a noble service and it was carried through in a fine spirit of love and fearlessness.

A great crisis arose in England in 1916 for those who held the absolutist peace position, of whom there were many in the Society of Friends. The Yearly Meeting, the Meeting for Sufferings and the Friends' Service Committee, rose to the emergency with much wisdom and courage. The messages which were issued were of a high order, and while there was a difference of opinion in the Quaker group, there was throughout a clear note of determination to keep the spiritual faith of the Society in its severest crisis. Many young Friends went to prison and bore their testimony in the face of hard suffering, scorn and danger.

This is not the place to set forth *in extenso* the fundamental grounds of the Quaker peace position. It has been many times interpreted and defended and the documents are at hand for those who wish them. This chapter is simply concerned to express the attitude and practice of the Society of Friends as a religious body and of the deeply concerned and seasoned members as individuals. It may take many years more of experience and suffering before the Christian world awakes universally to the truth that war and all its methods are absolutely incompatible with the teaching, the spirit, the kingdom and the way of life of our Lord and Master Jesus Christ. A prominent preacher said in the stress and strain of the Great War that he could imagine Christ sighting down the barrel of a rifle aimed at the enemy opposing the Allies and then firing it, and he further believed that if He were in the world to-day He would have called His followers to this fight. Well, Friends do not believe *that*, and they cannot be so swept off their calm faith in higher forces that they ever will believe it. They have not been as united on this absolutist peace position as some of us could wish and they have not been as effective in making their *idea* of life clear and attractive to men as they might have been. But this may perhaps be honestly and humbly said that the sound and solid kernel of the Society of Friends can under all conditions and circumstances be counted on as purveyors of peace and as peace-makers both in peace-time and war-time. They will not fight nor be entangled in the mechanisms of war. They will be calm and brave and heroic. They will not dodge their spiritual responsibilities, they will make heavy sacrifices to transmit their love, they will die if it will make their truth and faith dearer, but they will not endorse war-methods or support them or be themselves a voluntary part of a system that is engaged in carrying on war.

It may well be said that the world is not yet ready for this advanced idealism, that Christ Himself was filled with apocalpytic hopes, that He was proposing a programme for a new dispensation, not for this present mixed world. That may all be as it may be. But in any case, there ought to be a world like this one for which Christ lived and died. And that kind of a world will never actually come unless some of us take the vision and the hope seriously and set to work to make it real here on this very earth. It will be said again that these dreams and hopes are visionary and im-practical—even Christ Himself, with all His spiritual power and divine authority, failed to " change human nature ", came up against the thick bossed shield of fixed habit and ancient custom and ended His beautiful life in dark defeat and ignominious death. The answer is that He has been changing human nature ever since, that His Cross has become the most decisive factor in human history, and that it appears to be a better venture to die for love and truth and an ideal world than to live along the grooves of fixed habit and ancient custom and the old stupid compromise. The world will at least be better off if there is a Christian group, even a small one in England and America, resolved to live for these hopes, for this way of life, to bear their clear testimony for peace and love at any cost and at any price, and ready, if the last supreme sacrifice is demanded, to die for that faith and for that vision.

CHAPTER VIII

FRIENDS AND THE HUMANITARIAN SPIRIT

JOHN WILHELM ROWNTREE of York finished a moving address in the Manchester Conference in 1895 with this prayer: " Thou, O Christ, convince us by Thy Spirit, thrill us with Thy Divine passion, drown our selfishness in Thy invading love, lay on us the burden of the world's suffering, drive us forth with the apostolic fervour of the early Church ! "

He was at the time a young man of twenty-seven, the forward-looking leader of the younger section of the Society of Friends in England and a fresh and vital interpreter of its message for the new age. It was no accident that he emphasized two central notes: the invasion of the individual life by the Spirit of Christ, and the call for Friends to " take up the burden of the world's suffering ". These are two outstanding spiritual aims of Friends in all generations of their history, and the young prophet was merely calling his people to the tasks of life which his forerunners had recognized as most important.

Quakerism was born with a passion for a better social world. George Fox was not a monastic type of reformer. His thought did not centre upon inward thrills and personal deliverance. He was always concerned for those who suffered and were heavy-laden. The more clearly he saw the divine potentiality of man, the more tragic seemed the marring and spoiling of these human beings who were meant to have the joy and liberty of sons of God. The great agonies of his spirit—the burdens which broke his health and threatened his mental stability—were not over his own state of life but over what seemed to him the failure of the Church to follow Christ's way of life and over the miserable condition of the world around him. He had no quick remedy for the trouble, no easy panacea. " The seed of God reigning in the hearts of men " is always his answer. But that is not some dream of inward piety. When " the seed of God reigns " in a person, it makes him a Christlike man and sets him at the same spiritual tasks Christ Himself worked at, and it raises him into that same self-giving, sacrificing spirit that was in Him.

The priceless estimate of human life is everywhere in evidence in that early Quaker movement. " The publishers of truth ", as the itinerant missionaries of the first period were called, talked about the light of God in the soul and the new and larger freedom of life for every man. They attacked the prevailing forms of fashion and etiquette because they seemed hollow and unreal, but particularly because they hampered and belittled man and woman. They sensitively felt the horrors of drunkenness and sensuality because they saw in them living graves for men who ought to be joyous and free. They cried out against the appalling jails and prisons of their time, not because *they* found themselves so often incarcerated in them, but because they saw there, in a shocking revelation, the inhumanity and barbarity of man's treatment of man. They found them to be nests of disease and schools of crime and instruments of hate and vengeance, instead of being places for reforming and rebuilding those who had gone astray. Much of the moral evil in the world seemed to them to be due not so much to the inherent perversity of man's heart as to the social conditions of life in which children and adults were compelled to live. These Friends always held a brief for those who were the victims of ignorance and greed, for those who were " submerged ", and especially for the unfavoured and undeveloped races.

John Bellers was the first of the Quaker humanitarians to work out with care and insight the principles of a new philanthropy. He died in 1725, and his little pamphlets were written in the early part of that century and the closing years of the previous one. Karl Marx called him " a veritable phenomenon in the history of political economy ", but the more important point is his acute and creative Christian conscience. His tender spirit is revealed in his beautiful prayer appended to one of his essays : " Make us, O Lord, what is right in Thy sight, suitable to the beings which Thou hast made us and the stations which Thou hast placed us in, that our tables nor nothing that we enjoy may become a snare unto us ; but that the use and strength of all that we receive from Thy bountiful hand may be returned unto Thee." Bellers, in his simplicity of spirit and in the depth and wisdom of his insight, reminds us very much of John Woolman. One feels all the time like asking, How does it happen that this man knows, never having studied with the experts ? But his touch is sure and his words are always weighty.

In his *Essays about the Poor*, he says : " That the Poor want to be better managed than they are is plain to every one that hath sense or charity, whilst their

way of living is not much less Loss to the Nation than
our Wars, one being perpetual and the other but acci-
dental ; also the ill Morals and Miseries of the Poor
are scandalous to our Religion to the last Degree."
Again he writes : " It is a certain Demonstration of the
Illness of the Method the People are imploy'd in, if
they cannot live by it ; nothing being more plain than
that Men in proper Labour and Imployment are capable
of earning more than a living." Once more he declares :
" Land, Catel, Houses, Goods, Money are but Carcas
of Riches, they are dead without People ; Men being
the Life and Soul of them." " Traders may grow rich ",
he says, " whilst a Nation grows poor through extrava-
gancy, for when the Dealers may get 20 Thousand
Pound by Claret, the Nation pays and spends 100
Thousand Pound for it, and no Body grows Rich by
Drinking it, whatever the Seller doth." In his " Pro-
posals for raising a Colledge of Industry," he comments
upon the strange fact that the world is much more
careful about its methods of raising corn and cattle
than about its methods of *raising men*, and he points
out that " the present Idle Hands of the Poor of this
Nation are able to raise Provisions and Manufactures
that would bring England as much Treasure as the
Mines do Spain ".

John Woolman, of Mount Holly, New Jersey, is the
next spiritual genius to interpret the Quaker ideals of
human service. Long before he wrote that perfect
literary gem, his *Journal*, or his remarkable Tract, *A
Word of Remembrance and Caution to the Rich*, his life
had been giving visible illustration of the principles
which he so simply but impressively expounded. It is
always the palpitating tenderness of the man that
touches the reader most—the Franciscan love and

sympathy. He always felt that his love for suffering humanity was rooted in his own experience of the love and tenderness of God. " I was early convinced in my mind ", he says near the opening of the *Journal*, " that true religion consisted in an inward life wherein the heart doth love and reverence God the Creator and learns to exercise true justice and goodness not only toward all men, but also toward the brute creation ; that, as the mind was moved by an inward principle to love God as an invisible, incomprehensible Being, so by the same principle, *it was moved to love him in all his manifestations in the visible world.*" " *To say we love God as unseen, and at the same time exercise cruelty toward the least creature moving by his life, or by life derived from him, was a contradiction in itself.*" In a great illness once he seemed to hear the angels in heaven saying, " John Woolman is dead ", but he came back in his awakened consciousness to the discovery that he had died to an old self to be reborn to a new and more Christ-like self, and something like that transmutation really happened. In that same illness, when he was so near death that he forgot his own name, Woolman says, " I found myself fused in with a mass of matter of a dull gloomy colour between the south and the east, and was informed that this mass was human beings in as great misery as they could be and live ". " I was ", he continues in his restrained and humble style, " mixed with them and could not consider myself as a distinct or separate being. In this state I remained several hours." " I was then carried in spirit to the mines where poor oppressed people were digging rich treasures for those called Christians, and heard them blaspheme the name of Christ, at which I was grieved, for his name was precious.

I was then informed that these heathen were told that those who oppressed them were the followers of Christ, and they said among themselves, ' If Christ directed them to use us in this sort, then Christ is a cruel tyrant '." The vision seemed to him a real parable of life. He was merged in with those who suffered and he lost his own separate individuality, being part of the nameless group of toilers, and when he returned to life and consciousness, he felt himself dead to his own will but born into a new and Christ-like love for men.

His deepest concern on earth—after the purification of his own spirit—was the liberation and elevation of the people of colour on the American continent, the negroes and the Indians. Once more there came a John who was a " well beloved disciple "—a well beloved disciple of liberty. He felt himself to be bound with those who bore the chains of slavery. He felt himself to be a fellow sufferer with the humiliated and mistreated Indians. He did not see them as a spectator. He entered into their inner state and travail of soul. He shared their life. He pleaded their cause as though he were of their tribe and family. He saw, too, with the clear insight of a prophet the moral effect of negro slavery and of injustice to the Indian.

> He read each wound, each weakness clear;
> He struck his finger on the place
> And said, " Thou ailest here and here."

Always and everywhere his life and his words reveal his reigning sense of the preciousness of a human life. It is not merely the *soul* that is precious and that is to be " saved " for eternal bliss in a world beyond. The

life for him is precious here and now and must be freed
from its fardels and burdens and raised to its diviner
possibilities. His concern for the labourer, toiling
under wrong economic conditions and social handicaps,
is just as intense as for the negro chattel. Nor does
he confine his sympathy to the poor toiler. He is
fully as eager to liberate and enlarge the rich who are
as apt to miss the fullness of life as are the poor. The
problem is always deeper than economic categories.
It is not so much a question of wealth and poverty as
it is a question of spiritual health and inner freedom.
There is something little short of sublime in the story
of this humble saint walking from place to place in
England near the end of his life because his tender heart
would not allow him to ride in stage coaches or send
letters by them and so give his sanction to the prevailing ways of life which a selfish society of the time
prescribed for over-worked post-boys. In his last illness, his thoughts were not for himself or even for his
dearest friends ; they were still for unknown sufferers.
" I felt the depth and extent of the misery of my fellow
creatures, separated from the divine harmony, and it
was heavier than I could bear. . . . In the depths of
the misery, O Lord ! I remembered that thou art omni-
potent ; that I had called thee Father ; and I felt that
I loved thee, and I was made quiet in my will." He
said at the end that he was kept " steady and centred
in everlasting love ".

It will perhaps be said that one swallow does not
make a summer and one rare saint does not make a
holy people. It is quite true that not all the Friends
of the seventeenth century were John Woolmans. At
the same time, he was not a lone and solitary figure, a
spiritual alien and stranger in the Society to which he

K

belonged. There were many others who had a similar spirit and a tenderness not unlike his. John Churchman is almost in his class and so, too, is John Pemberton and others who were not named John. The dry old Minute Books of the time bear testimony to a noble faith in man and a living concern for his enlargement and betterment, and so, too, do many of the *Journals* of public Friends, both in England and America. Their lives spoke the same message of dedication, love and humility, though their pens could not make their ideal as articulate as Woolman did.

The great evangelical awakening in England had a deep and far-reaching effect on many members of the Society of Friends, especially upon some of the leading ministers of it. The influence came in the main through the evangelical movement within the Anglican Church rather than through the direct impact of the Wesleyan revival. There were a few Quaker ministers who caught the evangelical fervour before the Anglican influence did its work upon them. They were for the most part men and women who had come into the Society by convincement and who were not under the Quietist attitude of mind to quite the same extent that the " birthright " Friends usually were. Mary Dudley, an English Friend of large gifts, and Stephen Grellet, of noble French birth, who was convinced while in exile in America, are two ministers who did much to produce a new spiritual atmosphere without themselves being conscious of any change of religious outlook from their fellow members. William Savery, of Philadelphia, a " birthright " Friend, and David Sands, of New York, a " convinced " Friend, while remaining in both instances thoroughly loyal to the prevailing type of Quakerism in their day, nevertheless introduced unconsciously into their ministry a fresh appealing power and a livelier evangelical note of warmth and fervour.

With the new evangelical spirit came also a fresh and quickened devotion to human betterment. Evangelical religion is not seldom wrapped up in the one over-mastering aim to get men's souls saved for a blissful eternity after life in this vale of mutability is over. That one thing seems so tremendously important that everything else in the universe drops to a secondary plane, and too often persons swept by this intense faith have been inclined to leave human wrongs to right themselves and have been almost callous to the sufferings of little children and the sad inequalities of the social scale. That was not the case, however, with those who came under the spell of evangelical piety at the opening of the nineteenth century. William Wilberforce, Thomas Clarkson and Fowell Buxton are three shining examples of men who were stirred to an overaweing sense of the work of saving grace in their hearts and who at the same time were aroused with an irresistible passion to right the wrongs of humanity. It was through this little band of " evangelicals " and their friends of similar faith that certain sensitive Quaker souls were awakened to a large and momentous service for " the unhappy peoples " of the world. Joseph John Gurney, his sister Elizabeth Fry, Samuel Gurney (the famous London banker), William Allen (chemist and Fellow of the Royal Society), Joseph Sturge, William Forster, Samuel Tuke, and many another noble leader in the Society of Friends in those years were all swept by the powerful decuman wave of the evangelical movement. Quakerism had ploughed ruts and grooves for its currents of life to run in. It too often had set into dull formal moulds of custom. Its development was arrested and its marching power had waned. Once more, as at first, though in a quite different manner and with a different pushing force, the hot lava underneath burst through the framework and produced fresh movement and clearer world outlook, but as always happens in such cases, with some upheaval of the ancient ground and some destructive results.

The slave and the prisoner were the two focal centres of interest. It is not too much to say that it was the evangelical movement that ended the slave trade of Great Britain and then set free all the slaves in the British Colonies. The important result might possibly have come some other way and from the impact of some different moral driving-power, but as an actual fact of history, it came this way and from this driving-power. Elizabeth Fry, kindled and quickened by the same spiritual impact, turned her fervid current of love and devotion toward the amelioration of the intolerable condition of the men and women who lay, abject and hopeless, in the jails and prisons of England. She not only brought a new theory of penology and correction ; what was more important, she brought a new spirit and atmosphere. She made prisoners conscious that there was a human love which reached even to them, and through this unexpected human love, they rose to a fresh faith in the love and grace of God. The influence of William Savery on Elizabeth Fry's life and work was much greater than one used to suppose, but at the same time, behind and through all her transforming work there flowed a strong current of this molten lava of the evangelical movement. The extraordinary work of Stephen Grellet and William Allen, in

Russia and in other parts of Europe, shows the same heat and power, and Joseph Sturge and William Forster were both baptized with the same spirit and fire. The important thing to note in all this Quaker philanthropy of the era is its tenderness. It was not " charity " in the cold sense of the word. It was a love divinely begotten, a self-giving and sacrificial love. These humanitarian Friends wept with those that wept, agonized with those who suffered, and shared themselves with the slave, the poor, the prisoner, the unfriended and the outcast.

In America the wave of Quaker dedication to the cause of abolition came a little later than this great period of splendid English humanitarian service. The leaders in America were not to anything like the same degree affected by the evangelical movement. They were closer to the original current of Quaker life and thought. They were more nearly in the direct line of succession from George Fox, through Anthony Benezet and John Woolman. If we take Whittier, as we undoubtedly should, as the typical leader of the American Quaker movement, we have in him the true fruit and offspring of primitive, fundamental Quakerism. He felt the inner meaning and shared the deep spiritual insight of the first founders. His living experience was like theirs. His deep sense of the soul's direct relation to God was of a piece with theirs. He felt the immeasurable worth of man as they did. His spring and motive was a tender humble love like theirs. His two poems, " Eternal Goodness " and " Our Master ", are two of the best interpretations of genuine Quakerism that have ever been written. Those who were closest to him in the work during those discouraging years of ever-expanding slave territory, when no one could dream that the event of total release from bondage was so near, were in large measure in sympathy with his broad faith. Benjamin Lundy, Thomas Garrett, Levi Coffin, Thomas Shipley, Elizabeth Buffum Chace, Lucretia Mott, Daniel Neal, Isaac T. Hopper, William C. Taber, all had very simple and untheological religious faith and experience. They all had an unlimited faith in man's divine destiny and in his inalienable right to a free chance to realize that destiny on earth. They met opprobrium. They were jeered and hooted. They were threatened and pursued. They suffered loss and ill-fame. But they were absolutely sure that man's freedom was God's cause and that in the long run His truth would prevail.

It cannot, of course, be claimed that the slaves in America owed their freedom to the persistent work of the Quakers. Nothing even approaching that can be proved or rightly claimed. The Friends did, however, first through their gifted leaders and finally through the unified and importunate effort of almost the entire membership, drive the issue of abolition into the moral consciousness of the nation and arouse and stimulate those dynamic men who finally carried the cause through to its goal. The Friends never let go, never despaired, and all the time kept the torch moving on from hand to hand. When the victory came, in the unexpected way, by the besom of war, Friends rallied at once to the no less difficult task of helping to raise the former bondmen, the freedmen of Lincoln's proclamation, to their new level of life. Education for the immediate duties of life was the obvious need, and to this Friends gave themselves with zeal and with practical skill and with large generosity. This work for freedmen in the epoch following the Civil War is one of the signal instances when Friends took up " the burden of the world's suffering ".

While this piece of human service was still going on, President-elect Grant, in 1869, suddenly called upon the Friends of America to take the major part of the burden of caring for the higher interests of the tribal Indians of the United States. The story of this constructive work during President Grant's administration has been adequately told in Rayner W. Kelsey's *Friends and the Indians*, and does not need to be reviewed here. The point I am emphasizing is this historical fact, that Friends find it perfectly natural to become the helpers of these less-favoured peoples— less favoured, I mean, in privileges and opportunities— and they have always had the confidence and love of their darker coloured friends. Their contribution to the life and civilization of the Negroes and Indians, so far as it has been an important contribution, has been possible through their capacity to understand the mind and spirit of those who compose these two races, and through their readiness to share themselves in ways of love and fellowship with those whom they wished to help.

This feature of Quaker humanitarian service has found its largest expression during the years of the Great War and the period of reconstruction following it. Measured in terms of financial outlay, the Quaker relief, managed by English and American Friends, does not look very momentous. It would possibly have financed the war-operations of England or America for a single day during the period of deadliest conflict. But that is not the way to measure it. It has been a great practical experiment in the application of Christ's way of life and method of love. Dr. Richard Cabot of

Boston, now Professor in Harvard University, in a personal letter written at the time, has beautifully and vividly expressed in the following words how he felt about the spirit and devotion of the young Quaker workers whom he met in France : " We have hitched up our dispensary with the Quakers who are working in Paris and outside it for refugees in a spirit not equalled on the whole by any group I have seen out here. They work with their hands, build houses, help with the ploughing, do plumbing work when plumbers are unobtainable, sleep in quarters that others find too hard, save money everywhere, and because they know what simple living is, are the best of case workers in city charities, never pauperizing, never offending. They work in the true religious spirit, asking no glory and no position, sharing the hardships they alleviate, and earning everywhere such gratitude from the French that the Government has offered to turn over a whole department to them if they will undertake all the work of reconstruction there. Others working here in France have friends and enemies ; the Friends have only friends, and I hear only praise of their work and can give only praise from what I have seen." At first, in each country where the reconstruction and relief were carried on, the people who were being helped suspected some ulterior, subterranean motive. They could not seem to believe that it was pure, unalloyed friendship. They were on the watch for some subtle utilitarian scheme underneath. " Why did you come ? " they would ask. " What do you expect to get ? " They found it hard to be convinced that no toll was to be taken from them in some form or other. They said quite simply and naïvely, " People do not take risks like these, or work this way under such conditions of life, or spend large sums of money, unless they expect to get something back as an equivalent." Gradually they caught the spirit and felt the love and fellowship, and saw that there can be a way of life that is unselfish and that enjoys giving and sharing.

This way of life, when it was finally understood, made, perhaps, its deepest impression on the Germans and the Austrians. Their need and their suffering were the greatest and at the same time they had the least expectation of such help. It has not been customary for people of one " enemy country " to go to the aid of the suffering children in another " enemy country ". It would be well if it happened more often, and very likely it will happen in the future, if wars continue, but in the past it has not become a habit and therefore it came as a strange surprise. It soon touched the hearts of the recipients and it met a beautiful response. Mutual fellowship and friendship sprang out of the service, and even where the recipients were Roman Catholics, the affection and understanding mind were just as real and genuine as in Protestant sections. It is hard to believe that the children themselves whose lives were saved or nourished back to strength will ever forget the strangers from abroad who came to their rescue in the hour of need. One touching incident may do to illustrate the submerged feelings and attitudes of these children. A little boy came near being killed by an automobile one day in the streets of Frankfort and was rescued in the nick of the crisis by a man who at considerable risk to himself rushed into the street, caught the boy in his arms, and carried him to safety. When he got home, the boy told his mother that he would have been killed on his way from school if a kind Quaker had not leaped into the point of danger and caught him before the on-coming motor-car hit him. His mother asked him how he knew that it was a Quaker. "Why," the little boy answered in great simplicity, "I thought it was always Quakers who saved little children!"

One of the most humiliating things about it all has been that the appreciation throughout Europe has outrun the contribution that was made. The messengers of the love and service have been idealized and their deeds have been "projected" to a pinnacle quite beyond the cold facts. One has often been reminded of what the peasant said to St. Francis of Assisi: "Try to be as good as all men believe thou art!" The faith and expectation which have been raised in the minds of these men and women and children of Europe furnish a powerful spur to every genuine Quaker to meet that faith and not to allow that expectation to suffer disillusionment. There are few woes more to be dreaded than that woe which falls upon those of whom "all men speak well", and who nevertheless do not have the inherent qualifications of life to warrant the exalted estimate. Time, as so often is the case, is the impartial judge and there is no appeal from its days of final judgment.

Friends have taken during recent years a prominent part with others in inaugurating plans and methods for cultivating a closer and happier mutual relation between the owners and managers of large business operations and those who are employed as labourers in them. George Cadbury, the builder of Bourneville, and Joseph Rowntree, who founded New Earswick, were both dedicated to the best interest and welfare of the men and women who were employed in their two extensive cocoa-works.

The model villages are well known and have had far-reaching influence on similar experiments elsewhere. But far more important than the creative work which remains for the social expert to study was the remarkable spirit of love and kindness which characterized these two men. Behind all they did that is still visible and tangible, there was an invisible aura and atmosphere which all workers felt and to which they always responded.

We have seen that John's Gospel substitutes for the story of the Last Supper, with its sacramental significance, the story of Christ washing His disciples' feet, and adding the injunction, " You are to wash one another's feet ", and " You are to love *even as* I have loved you ". This is another type of sacrament—a sacrament which requires the officiation of no ordained minister, but which can be performed in spirit and truth only by those who have felt " the mighty ordination of the pierced hands ". Friends, not only in this period of world tragedy, but for two hundred and fifty years, have felt a solemn call of the Master to live and act in that sacramental service. " Washing feet " has meant to them, not a ceremony for Maundy Thursday once in the year, but a continuous work of love and humility applied wherever there are bruised and tired feet of toilers. St. Augustine declared that Christians tend God's head but neglect His feet, and Walter Hilton, the English mystic of the fourteenth century, said in a similar vein : " Surely He will more thank thee for the humble washing of His feet, when they are very foul and yield an ill savour to thee, than for all the curious painting and fair dressing or decking that thou canst make about His head by devoutest remembrance ". This foot-washing of the known and unknown disciples of the Lord Friends have tried to do, and that must still be their mission if they are to continue to deserve their name of " Friends ".

William James said in his *Varieties of Religious Experience* that Quakerism is " a religion of veracity, rooted in spiritual inwardness ". But it would be a mistake to emphasize " inwardness " as though it were something opposed to " outwardness ". The Quakers have turned their attention to the inner life in order that they might be more truly effective when they turn to the work of the outward world. Their religion is like the diastole and systole of the heart by which the blood is drawn to the centre, purified and sent out again to construct and rebuild the tissue for the work of the world. In Isaiah's vision of the perfect worshipper the prophet saw him veil his face with two of his wings as a sign of reverence and adoration in the hushed presence of the Lord, but with two of his wings he was waiting to fly abroad for service, the moment the call came for it. This harmonious union of the outer and the inner life is a characteristic Quaker trait.

There is a great tendency to-day to work out a new abstract scheme for a better social order. It is plain enough that the order needs to change and that a new order is a thing greatly to be desired. But the Friend's main concern is not the floating of a new social scheme in the abstract. He cares much more for the exhibition of a truer and more humane spirit and way of life brought into living operation. Some day no doubt the new and better order of society will be formulated and will be put into exact scientific shape, but before that can happen there must be experiments tried, ways of life tested out and many practical attempts made to bring the lives of men into happier and more harmonious order. These experiments in love and fellowship, these attempts to show that the kingdom of God is already here *among us*, is a serious part of the faith and practice of the Quakers.

CHAPTER IX

FRIENDS' LEADERSHIP IN EDUCATION

ONE might have supposed that a religious Society built around the principle of an inward light would have discounted the necessity for education. But that was not what actually happened. Something almost diametrically the opposite to that really happened, as we shall see. There have always been some few Friends in every period who have been inclined to take the easy way and who have been ready to say that the Spirit will guide His people into all the truth. It used to be said in a certain rural meeting, when an ignorant itinerant minister came on a visit: " Now we shall get the pure gospel, for John has never been spoiled by book-learning ". No doubt individual Friends have had a fear of study and of learning, and here and there a particular Friend has over-strained the expectation of having information supplied from within, without the necessity of toiling or spinning. On one occasion, when the Elders in a Philadelphia meeting took a minister to task for having misquoted a text of Scripture in his sermon, he answered with authority: " I gave it as it was ' given ' to me ! " That would be a very handy way of arriving at the truth for which we seek, and we *might* have been favoured with such a plan of transmission. But the way our world is made did not apparently include this

easy acquisition of information. Browning has his
Paracelsus declare that " Truth is within ourselves ", and
he adds that

> To know,
> Rather consists in opening out a way
> Whence the imprisoned splendour may escape,
> Than in effecting entry for a light
> Supposed to be without.

Friends, however, have not given much aid and
comfort to that extreme view. Just because they saw
how easy it would be for their principle of the Light to
be exaggerated and raised to a kind of magic—like
the use of Aladdin's lamp—Friends have shown peculiar
zeal to exalt the importance of education. George Fox
felt his own lack of equipment and welcomed into his
fellowship men like William Penn, Robert Barclay,
Alexander Jaffray, Thomas Ellwood and others of
good scholarly training. He always showed a zeal
for education and did much to promote it at home
and abroad. He secured the establishment in 1668 of
two schools, one for children at Waltham Abbey and
one at Shacklewell, " set up to instruct young lasses
and maidens in whatsoever things was civil and useful
in creation ". Thomas Lawson, one of the earliest
Quaker schoolmasters, in a letter printed in *Quaker
Post-Bag*, tells of a project which George Fox and
William Penn had " to purchase a piece of land near
London for the use of a garden school-house . . . so
that children in the city could have a chance to study
nature " and grow up in the knowledge of the Lord and
His creation and so become " true philosophers ! "
George Fox wrote these wise and comprehensive words
of advice to his fellow members : " See that school-
masters and mistresses who are faithful Friends and

well qualified be placed and encouraged in all cities and great towns and where they may be needed: the masters to be diligent to forward their scholars in learning and in the frequent reading of the Holy Scriptures and other good books, that being thus *seasoned with the truth,* sanctified to God and taught our holy, self-denying way, they may be instrumental to the glory of God and the generation ". One of the first provisions for the care of Monthly Meetings over their members was " to help parents in the education of their children ". From almost the very first the Quaker school became an adjunct of the meeting and the teaching-master as important a figure as the minister. William Penn put education on a very high plane both in his own family and in his colony. In his famous letter to his wife and children he urges " liberal learning ", and in his *Fruits of Solitude* he has much to say about the importance of study and mental culture. Still more significant was his *action* in the matter. He founded and chartered a school in his new colony which has had an unbroken career of service until the present time. It is one of the oldest continuous schools in America.

Wherever Quakerism spread through the American Colonies a Quaker school sprang up in the forest alongside of the meeting house. It is not easy to overestimate the effect of these little pioneer schools upon the lives of the Quaker children. These children usually received an oversight and nurture which other children in the region too often missed. In some instances others besides Friends were admitted to the Quaker school, but for the most part the religious motive was so prominent that the school was felt to be a nursery for Quaker plants. As a result of these little centres of education in the colonial period, Friends maintained a high level of spiritual and intellectual life, even in backwoods districts, and itinerant ministers on their travels " to promote truth " were often surprised to find a good degree of breadth and depth in the rural Quaker flocks. There are many Quaker *Journals* from the eighteenth century, written by public Friends whose entire lives were lived on farms, remote from centres of culture and who nevertheless show large and spacious minds, conversant with the serious issues of life and who in range of thought were well abreast of the educated men and women of their time. They often revealed a grace and charm which was rare and beautiful and which was due in some measure to their form and type of education—as John Woolman expressed it, " glances of real beauty may be seen in their faces ".

This primitive stage of Quaker education was too exclusive and too much designed for their own chosen seed, but it had an immense shaping influence upon the children of the Society. The leaders of the flock in that century were timid, withdrawn from the world and concerned for the propagation of their own peculiar religious faith, and they carefully worked out an educational method which would accomplish what they had most at heart. That particular aim these little schools admirably fostered, and in the quiet retreats the children of the meeting were shaped and moulded into the pattern of their fathers and mothers and were prepared to take up the mantles of their forerunners as death called the latter from the scenes of their labours. Gradually many of these schools widened out to a larger community service in their neighbourhoods, taking in and training others besides Friends, and in

L

some sections of the country the pioneer Quaker schools formed the nucleus of the school system of the county or even for the State. The oldest public school in New York City was originally a Quaker colonial school, and in many districts of Ohio, Indiana, Iowa and Kansas, the leading public schools have blossomed out of the plant which the pioneer Quakers started.

If, with their passion for quiet training-places for their young children, the early Quakers had also had the insight to build an institution of higher learning, as the Puritan Colonists did at Harvard and at Yale, the course of Quaker history would have been a different story. There would have been a group of trained leaders who could have met the various Quaker crises with more intelligent guidance and with broader outlook. There would almost certainly have been no separation in 1827, and the Quakers would have made a larger contribution to the civic life of the country and to the religious thought of the nineteenth century. It was not strange that no one saw the full importance of such an institution in the early Quaker period. At first, the Quakers were in the throes of a fierce persecution and had to win their right to live and to worship. They could hardly have been expected to aim at the luxury of higher education until they reached a stage of comparative leisure. The Puritans felt that their essential existence hung upon having a training place for the preparation of ministers. There was a drive of spiritual necessity behind the founding of Harvard College. The Quakers felt no such necessity for the training of ministers.

What they ought to have desired, no doubt, was the adequate education of the entire membership so that any man or woman who might be called to be an organ of the Spirit would be ready for his life of spiritual service. The Quaker principle, properly understood, called for fearless education, since there is no safety in individualism, in personal responsibility, or in democracy, whether in civil or religious matters, unless every individual is given a chance to correct his narrow individualism in the light of the experience of larger groups of men. If a person is to be called upon to follow " his Light ", he must be helped to correct his subjective seemings by the gathered objective wisdom of the race, as expressed in scientific truth, in historical knowledge, in established institutions and in the sifted literature of the world. The Quaker ideal of ministry of all things calls for a broad and expansive education. If the particular sermon is not to be definitely prepared, then surely the person who is to minister must *himself* be prepared. If he is to avoid the repetition of his petty notions and commonplace thoughts, he must form a richer and more comprehensive experience from which to draw. We see all these implications clearly enough now, but they did not rise to the force of compelling insight in the sterner colonial days.

Many of the early schools, however, like Penn's Chartered School in Philadelphia, and like some of the best in London and Bristol and in other parts of England and Ireland, had a broad curriculum of studies and employed teachers of sound learning and large scholarship. Besides this, the wealthier English Friends and many, too, of the best colonial families, had tutors for their sons and daughters, so that, though it was rare for a Friend to have the advantages of university training (in England it was impossible by fixed restrictions of the universities themselves), there were, nevertheless, both men and women to be found in Quaker circles who were intellectually quite the equals of the men who were adorned with degrees. Sixteen Quakers were chosen to be Fellows of the Royal Society before the year 1825. A type of education which produced John Dalton, who formulated the chemical atomic theory ; William Allen, chemist and philanthropist ; Dr. John Fothergill, distinguished physician, educator and friend of Benjamin Franklin ; Luke Howard, one of the founders of meteorology and friend of Goethe ; Lindley Murray, the great grammarian ; William Rotch, ship-master and advocate of the divine Light in the human soul before the French Assembly in the early days of the Revolution ; and Moses Brown, great manufacturer, philanthropist and promoter of education, has much to be said for it.

The last quarter of the eighteenth century saw a remarkable expansion of Quaker education. The new step was marked by an *awakening* of the leaders of the Society to the immense importance of education for the enlargement of life, personality and service. Dr. John Fothergill was the leader of the movement, but he had a splendid group of helpers in England and there were Friends of like spirit at work in different parts of the American field. In 1779 the first of the large Quaker boarding schools was opened at Ackworth in Yorkshire, and its creation was an immediate stimulus to other localities. In 1784 a similar project was launched in New England under the leadership of Moses Brown, and a boarding school was opened that year in Portsmouth, Rhode Island, of which the present Moses Brown School in Providence is the successor. In 1796 New York Yearly Meeting set up Nine Partners Boarding School at Washington, in the State of New York, of which the present Oakwood Seminary at

Poughkeepsie is the successor. In 1799 Philadelphia Friends established their great school on a six-hundred acre tract of land at Westtown, about twenty miles from Philadelphia. Sidcot School in Somerset followed in 1808, a development and evolution from earlier educational ventures in the western counties of England. Irish Friends were not a bit behind their fellow members in England and America, so that by the opening of the nineteenth century Friends were well equipped for the education of their own membership. It should be said that at this stage Friends had not caught the vision of their mission as educators for the spiritual life and service of the world. They still thought of their new boarding schools as nurseries of Quakerism. They maintained what they were pleased to call a system of " guarded education ". They thought of these schools as homes of nurture for their own children and they designed them as training places for those who were to be a " peculiar people ". The children were guarded from the temptations and contaminations of the world. Like the ancient children of Israel, they lived " under rules and regulations ". They were kept to " plainness " in speech and dress. They were kept from all books and magazines that could poison their minds. They had no fiction, no drama, no music. What they did do was to learn a few things pretty well down to the bottom. They could read and write and spell, and they knew their English grammar and their mathematics as one knows the familiar scenes of his birthplace.

They lived all the time in the warm atmosphere of the Quaker spirit and practice. They heard the Bible read every day and sat in the deep stillness that followed the reading. They had two Quaker meetings a week. They were given good, full measure in length, and they heard not only their own gifted Friends, but they heard also the numerous visiting ministers who came in a pretty continuous stream from all parts of the earth where there were Quaker members. There were some who wearied of the narrow life, with its forcing methods of piety, but the general effect was constructive and wholesome. Out of these schools came the leaders of the Society and the men and women who carried the Quaker ideals into the social and spiritual tasks of the time.

But it was, nevertheless, a contracted and restricted life and it missed some of the finest features of an all-round education. Gradually, as the last century progressed, Friends came to feel that they had a larger educational mission than that of making Quakers of their own offspring. At first the new and broader ideas were met with opposition and they made their way slowly. Little by little, however, the fences and hedges began to disappear. Peculiarities ceased to count. Men and women of vision, with pedagogical training and with that indefinable power of arousing love and confidence in boys and girls, came to the leadership of the Quaker schools and parents who were not Friends began to knock at the doors for the admission of their children.

The first important experiment in popular education in Great Britain was made by a Quaker, Joseph Lancaster (1778–1838). He was an eccentric person and an odd genius, but his contribution to the development of public education is none the less an important one. He began his educational experiment in 1801 in London, where he opened a school for all who wished to come, with a slight fee for those who could pay it, and none for the very poor. He employed the older pupils to teach the younger ones and he himself furnished the oversight, guidance and enthusiasm. He toured the country, lecturing on education, writing pamphlets to explain his scheme and awakened the apathetic public. The king, George III, became keenly interested in his plans, and some of the most distinguished persons of the time gave him backing and support. William Allen of Spitalfields, always ready to help any cause that promised to elevate human kind, assisted him, together with other sympathetic Friends, to found " The Royal Lancastrian Society for Promoting the Education of the Children of the Poor. " Out of this Society and its successor developed the first important system of public elementary education for the labouring classes of England. The board schools, which were the fruit of Lancaster's unflagging efforts, opened a door for the lower and most needy section of society, but still no proper provision was yet made for the public education of the children of the middle classes.

William Edward Forster endeavoured to meet this need in his famous Education Act of 1870. He was at the time Minister of Education. He was born and bred a Friend, son of the well-known Quaker minister and philanthropist, William Forster, though the distinguished educational leader was at the time no longer a member of the Society. He had an intense love for children and he was determined to open the way for the education of every child in Great Britain. His Bill was fiercely attacked both by extreme churchmen and by extreme dissenters, as it failed to satisfy the religious demands of either wing, but with all its limitations the new Act marked an epoch in the slow development of universal public education.

The next important step in the education of the working classes of England in which Friends took a leading part was the building up of the Adult Schools. Adult School work had a long uneventful period of evolution before Friends awoke to discover their own distinct " call " to this service. Adult classes for the study of the Bible were formed not long after Robert Raikes established his first " Sunday schools " in 1782. The most famous of these early adult classes were those started in Nottingham in 1798. The idea spread and many towns had classes or schools in operation before Friends had any large place in the work. The epoch-making step in the movement was the founding of the Severn Street Adult School in Birmingham in 1845 by Joseph Sturge. He was one of those rare and wonderful men who put a whole life and a radiant spirit behind each thing they undertake. His first aim was to reach and influence the boys of Birmingham, but unexpectedly men came as well as boys, and by 1852 the Adult School proper became differentiated and was launched upon its momentous career. In 1847 Joseph Sturge invited Quaker teachers from all parts of England to a conference on Bible teaching. Out of this conference the Friends' First-day School Association came to birth the same year, with Joseph Storrs Fry of Bristol as honorary secretary. The next important event in the development was the coming of William White to Birmingham, and the dedication of his life to the Adult School movement. When he began his work in Birmingham there were possibly five hundred men and women in adult classes ; when he died fifty years later there were fifty thousand members in the Adult Schools of England.

There was from 1860 onward a steady growth of

the movement and a parallel internal development of the idea. Beside the early morning classes for study and discussion, meetings for worship for the men and their families were added. These meetings had some features of a Friends' meeting. There were periods of silence, and a large degree of freedom of utterance for all in attendance, though some one person was generally asked to read a passage of Scripture and give an opening address. As the movement progressed it developed numerous social and economic features, and furnished the members with the mutual advantages of a well-organized club, while, unlike many clubs, it ministered effectively to the higher life of the membership.

As the work unfolded, the Adult School became in large measure an unsectarian working-man's church, developing the gifts of multitudes of men and women, training Christian workers, forming a corporate spirit of brotherhood, enlarging the mental life of the fellowship, and making the practical religion of the Gospels a real factor in the homes and the lives of the labourers of Great Britain. It has been in many ways, both in spirit and practice, like the " Tertiaries " of the Franciscan Brotherhood. It has not been a new sect, it has been a new fellowship, and a new attempt to carry the practical religion of Christ into actual operation.

In the second quarter of the nineteenth century there came a new educational awakening and some of the foremost Quaker institutions had their birth from this period. Bootham School for boys and the Mount School for girls were established in York, England, at this time—Bootham in 1823 and the Mount in 1831—and on the other side of the ocean Haverford College was founded near Philadelphia in 1833. In 1837 New Garden Boarding School, which later emerged into

Guilford College, was opened in North Carolina, and in 1847 a boarding school was established at Richmond, Indiana, which eventually became Earlham College. During the nineteenth century there were no less than eighty-five Quaker schools in England, five in Ireland and somewhat over fifty in America. There were at the end of that century nine Quaker colleges in America and one in Canada. Meantime three prominent Quakers of large wealth had founded three educational institutions which stand in quality at the top of American institutions of higher learning: Cornell University at Ithaca, New York; Johns Hopkins University in Baltimore, Maryland, and Bryn Mawr College for women at Bryn Mawr, Pennsylvania.

This list of institutions is an impressive evidence of activity, but it does not tell the real story of the Quaker contribution. That is something which cannot easily be told. The most important thing about any institution is not what meets the eye and can be revealed to the senses. It is the subtle, elusive, indefinable aspect, the invisible spirit and atmosphere of the institution. When the " holy city " is measured, it is in terms of cubits " according to the measure of a man, *that is, of an angel* ". When we measure the power and range of an educational institution the cubits of the measuring rod must be those of an angel. These Quaker schools and colleges to an observer who sees only the outside are precisely like any other set of well-planned and well-built schools and colleges. Some of them have architectural beauty and some of them are unadorned and commonplace, but almost without exception they have a peculiar inner life and an intangible spiritual power.

The thing that has marked Quaker education during

its modern period has been its *formative spiritual influence*. There has usually been little difference between the pedagogy in a Quaker school and that in any other good school. The Quaker teacher possesses no " secret " by which he can make it easier to learn geometry or to read Cæsar. It would perhaps be true that there is an unusual emphasis put upon being exact with information and with reports. The student is expected *to know what he knows*. He is trained to revere and respect the truth. He is taught to shun and avoid loose habits of thought and he is accustomed to observe and describe the actual facts under consideration. But all that is true of any good school or college. It can only be said that Friends as teachers have raised these characteristic features of sound education to an unusually high level and therefore they have been able to produce a large vintage of excellent scholars.

But the point that stands out as the hall-mark of Quaker education is a quality of life. A boy with a brilliant mind and tenacious memory can get a good education in almost any school or college. In fact, it is hard to keep him from getting it. He pushes forward, he gathers facts from every bush, he stocks his mind, he trains his powers of reasoning, and by what seems almost like magic, he leaps to an intellectual height which some other boy would never reach, even in the best school in the world. The fact, therefore, that a certain school turns out a striking crop of scholars may only mean that it has excellent material to work upon. It has not had to face the task of trying to " make silk purses out of sows' ears ". The surer test of a school is its power to mould the rank and file of its boys into harmoniously ordered lives. Here again some boys are much easier to " harmonize " and

" order " than others are. Robert Collyer used to say that " the amount of divine grace that would make a saint out of John wouldn't keep Peter from knocking a man down ! " When all the variations are taken into account, it may honestly be said, I think, that the Quaker educators have shown a rare capacity for this highest of all operations, the task of rightly fashioning the will and the character of youth.

It is not easy to single out the methods or the traits that have been peculiarly efficacious. We are forced once more to use that loose and over-worked word " atmosphere ". There is in any case a subtle *aura* which pervades an institution and which works unconsciously on a boy's life. The *spirit of the school* is just as real a thing as is the playing field. No one can quite define it, and a boy can hardly put it into words, but he feels it, responds to it and is shaped by it. The ideals of the place are as much a fact as the landscape is and every boy sooner or later feels their silent pull. An older fellow says to a newer boy, who proposes to do something unworthy of the place, " No, that doesn't go here ; we never do that sort of thing in this school." Other things being equal, the school where high ideals are silently working in class-rooms, on the playing field, in the dormitory ; where there is a strong community spirit and where through the years loyalty has been created in the minds of all the boys, is by far the best school and it is likely to have the best product in personality.

One advantage which the good Quaker school offers is its cultivation of the inner spirit of the student while his mind is being trained. This is so obviously a desideratum of education that one might suppose it would be a feature of any school, and in a loose way it probably is a vague aim and ideal of most schools, but the achievement of it is so difficult and it calls for such a combination of favouring factors that it is often crowded out and missed altogether. I cannot claim that all Quaker schools and colleges succeed in cultivating the deeper life, but it can at least be said that they all take that aspect of education seriously. They do not try or wish to push any sectarian interests and no attempt is made by any of these institutions, nor is any desire felt, to make Quaker " converts " of the students. What is done is to make the fundamental features of the religious life as *real* as possible. I say " religious life " advisedly. Religion is brought over from the abstract to the concrete, from definitions to practice. It is dealt with as a way of living, as something to be *done*, and not merely something to be talked about and left in the region of theory and speculation.

The student in a Quaker institution quickly feels that he is in an atmosphere of sincerity. The deeper issues of life are honestly met. No attempt is made to force upon him a religious position which conflicts with his scientific knowledge. The difficulties are squarely faced and considered and where possible a deeper interpretation found that makes reconciliation possible. I have a personal vivid memory of how a wise teacher in one of these schools led me through the difficulties which assaulted my faith when I was first confronted by the new facts of geology and biology, and how another wise guide helped me to find the way in college, when I was going through the mazes of psychology and philosophy. Nothing would have worked but honesty and straightforwardness. I felt the sanity of the leadership. I came over from an artificial theory of Scripture to a much more profound and vital conception of it—one that has stood me through life and has been a growing comfort to me as the years have run their course.

Another thing of immense importance in these institutions is the intimate fellowship which exists between the teachers and those who are taught. The best way to make religion real is to become a friend of a person whose religion is the fibre of his life and the fragrant perfume of his character.

Religion, then, does not rest on arguments and is not a thing of logic, but it is its own evidence and verification. These institutions are well known for their order and discipline. They expect to form habits that will be of lasting value, and they do not hold the view that whatever a boy or girl *likes to do* is what is right for him or her to do. But at the same time great stress is laid on the cultivation of confidence and understanding instead of force, and no one feels that the institution has done its work well unless a spirit of love and co-operation has been formed between teachers and students.

All Friends' institutions hold meetings for worship where all the students have an opportunity to experience the reality of worship. There is something vital about community silence which almost every one *feels*, and young people almost invariably, with very little explanation, enter into it appreciatively. These periods of hush have an important educational value, but they mean much more than that. They assist the serious youth to find himself, to discover his soul, to learn to meditate, to deepen his life, and many of the group in these quiet times become aware of the reality of God. They come away from their short periods of communion with new convictions, with clearer vision, with fresh power to resist temptation. It often means more in retrospect than while they are living through the experiences. Persons who have had these times of hush in Quaker institutions very often speak of them with deep appreciation in later life and look back on them as epochs in their journey. The whole tendency, I think it may be said, of this type of education is to establish faith and confidence in the religion of the Spirit. Teachers are but men and women, they are frail and human, and they do not always succeed, but their aim in these institutions is to lay the foundations of character, to train fine loyalties, to give nurture to a vital religion of life and to make the Life and Spirit of God real and vital as an energy in daily life.

There is no mission that has opened to the Society of Friends more important or more effective service than its varied forms of education. It reaches a vast number of young people through this means, and for the most part it helps them to find a pathway of life that leads forward and upward, and that enriches the whole journey with faith and truth and love.

CHAPTER X

THE NEW SPIRIT AND THE NEW WORLD

I HAVE no interest in sectarianism. I am not concerned to defend, or to propagate, the peculiarities of a sect. In what has been said as historical interpretation in previous chapters, I have been preparing the way for a forecast of the new worlds to be conquered.

There will always be among us so-called *realists*, conservative-minded persons, entrenched in the *status quo*, who insist that human nature is just "human nature". It cannot be changed. One might as well expect, these disciples of the Preacher in *Ecclesiastes* would say, to see figs growing on crab-apple trees as to expect to see human instincts transformed from egoist urges into social and co-operative influences. "What has been is what will be, and there is nothing *new* under the sun." For a human dreamer to "project" a new kind of world and spin ideals out of his head is as absurd as for an amœba to try to conjure up a paradise out of the slime of its mud puddle.

It may just possibly turn out that the "realist" is the "dreamer", that he is the one who is "projecting", and not dealing with facts. Somehow the world has gone up and forward from the single-cell, amœba-type of life to our complicated human type. And very much of the progress, at least in the last stages of advance, has been due to some one's power to forecast.

Certain ideals have proved to be efficacious. They have
been dynamic. They have worked. They have pulled
groups of people forward. Not all ideals, of course,
are constructive. Some are futile dreams. Ideals
must be tested and sifted like other forces. But when
the time is ripe for it and the mental climate is
favourable, a forward-reaching ideal lifts like a mag-
netized giant crane. These cranes have a lifting arm
charged with magnetic energy and they unload steel
rails by mere contact. You see the heavy rail rise from
its freight car and swing over to its new place without
any grip or tie, with no *hold* but an invisible attraction.

These fresh lifting ideals emerge out of individual
and social experience somewhat as " mutations "
emerge in the biological series. These " mutations "
may be just chance " sports " with no futurity, or
they may be new forms that lift the entire order of
life to higher levels. In any case they are " new " and
unpredictable, and having come, they must forthwith
stand the tests of struggle and survival. So, too, ideals
arrive here in a world that did not expect them. They
" break in " through some prophet-spirit, some leader,
who has a vision for the next step in the forward march
of the race. Usually, if the prophet is a real leader,
he possesses a rare gift of sensitiveness to feel, like
the migrating bird, the forward-pointing *direction*. He
does not exactly " create " the ideal. It is truer to
say that he discovers it. He feels the onward tendency
of the age. He catches the vague hopes of his forerunners. He draws to a focus many unfulfilled aspirations and desires. He becomes the living organ of aims
and purposes which till then have been abortive. He
tries out his ideal and finds that it lifts others. It
dynamizes kindred spirits. It produces *faith*. It

M

organizes a "group". It makes a centre of energy. And, if conditions are right and the ideal is an efficacious one, before long a certain part of the human race has come up to a new level and has launched a new way of living, somewhat as the attraction of the moon lifts an immense plateau of the ocean, directly under it, twenty-five feet higher than the surrounding water.

It should be said, however, that this new human level is reached, not by flying in the face of the facts of heredity, nor by eliminating instincts. Instincts are very queer things. To many persons they are mysterious entities. These persons talk about instincts in the same awesome manner that they talk about the "law" of evolution as if the "law" were the pushing or the steering force. Instincts are merely characteristic tendencies which can be either furthered or blocked by favouring or hindering circumstances. Whether the child shall grow up with no fear of furry animals or with an almost stupid terror of them will depend on the accidents of the early experiences. If he is bitten as a result of early contacts with animals or if he hears a disturbing noise which he associates with them, he will form a fear-habit that may last through life. On the other hand, if he meets no untoward circumstance, he will play on with rats and snakes and toads and baby bears in perfect peace, like the little child in Isaiah, that plays about the hole of the asp or the cockatrice's den !

Instincts are tendencies, potential energies, which can be organized and directed in a multitude of ways. Left to react in unordered and undirected ways, an egoistic instinctive tendency will *set* into a habit and can easily become an almost unalterable way of acting.

But that same tendency could equally well be " sublimated ", could be fused with other instincts and emotions and formed into a larger system of interest, changed over into a sentiment or a loyalty and become a driving force in some noble co-operative aim. There are few blinder dogmas than the theory that instincts commit the world to one old, undeviating track. It is a heresy, worse than that of Arius, that we are bound to sit by as silent spectators and watch " instincts " and " laws of heredity " drive the race round and round in the ancient circular course.

We may take it as a sound working principle that new forward " tracks " for humanity can be built and new " courses " of life can be formed, if we learn how to bring creative ideals into operation upon the youth of the world in their plastic stage of development. The question, for instance, whether one is to live under the drive of egoistic aims, or is to be dedicated to social and co-operative ends, is largely settled by the habits of thought that are formed in the early years of life and by the way the instincts and emotions are organized under dominating systems of interest and cultivated through day-by-day activities. One of these alternatives is no more " natural " than the other one is. Sacrifice and self-giving can easily become so completely second-nature that one does not " stop to think ", but gives himself in the same spontaneous fashion as when the miser risks himself to save his gold. It is a question which ideal becomes prepotent. In one case action along the line of least resistance has been cultivated and a narrow egoistic habit-path has been ploughed. In the other case the fundamental native interest in the life and welfare of others has been cultivated until pity, love and sympathy are the ruling " urges " to action. A person can carry either *stock of goods*. It will depend on how he " stocks up " at the period when the supply of life-interests are laid in.

What is true of these two alternatives is equally true of our general world-outlook. Shall we think of our universe as a materialistic, mechanistic system, or as a living, growing, creative, spiritual realm, with purposive Mind and loving Heart at the deepest centre of it ? It will depend on which system of thought is organized in our minds during the long formative period of education. Either one of these alternative systems of thought is arrived at by an extensive process of selection and elimination. If attention is continually focused upon one set of aspects with which the universe constantly bombards us, the facts which concern the other aspect gradually fall into the background and are eventually treated as negligible. Or *vice versa*, if the second set of aspects are played up and brought to focal prominence, then the facts that fail to fit this system of interest will drop out of our purview and will be inadequately dealt with. We are not " born " either " materialists " or believers in a realm of Spirit ; we are rather born with mental capacities for organizing our experiences of the world under either rubric. Which one prevails and finally becomes our working " complex " will depend on the formation of our habits of selection and on the way we have built our prepotent system of interest. In either case, we shall overlook and neglect many facts which are allowed to fall to low-level importance, because they do not fit our system of thought and interest ; that is to say, our " complex ". Some time—in the far future of the race—no doubt, men will discover how to gather these alternative systems into a single wider unity. They will be able to explain both aspects through a deeper organizing truth, but then, almost certainly a new pair of alternatives will emerge to bother the growing youth of that remote generation.

I have said enough, I hope, to make my main point clear. It is this, that the world progresses through the formation of an enlarging ideal of life, which in the first instance is the vision of a prophet. Then his vision dynamizes a group of disciples who are " loyal " to that ideal and it becomes the way of life and the driving force of a group or " team " of many members. And then if the ideal fits the higher needs of the race it slowly wins its way and becomes a dominant system of thought and action. Some of the purer and nobler aspects of the original ideal—some of the features which are too " ideal " for everyday human life—are likely to drop away, or be " compromised " and " adjusted ", as the circle of the group widens. But nevertheless large masses of men will in this manner be lifted to higher levels as the ideal wins its way and becomes a wide-spread principle of life and action.

The Quaker movement is historically one of these group-systems. At its heart and centre there is a dominant ideal—a vision of a world that ought to be. It has been an attempt to practise and to spread a *spirit, a way of life,* and to cultivate a group dedicated to that aim. The phrase " a spirit " is, of course, loose and vague. It needs to be interpreted. It amounts to what I have been calling " a system of interest ". This group of people is trying to demonstrate the fact that Christ's Galilean programme is a way of life which " works " better at least than any other one does. Its essential aspects are : faith in God as Father, faith in man as a potential son of God, and faith in the growing sway and kingdom of God on earth ; faith in the creative and conquering power of *love* as a method of life with our fellows ; faith in the attempt to understand men sympathetically; faith in an appeal to the higher diviner possibilities in men, and faith in the final effect of the co-operative and self-giving spirit. This is, no doubt, an optimistic programme ; so also was Christ's programme of life. There are, however, ugly opposing facts to be faced. There is admittedly a sad amount of human wreckage. Thugs and bandits are as much a reality in our world as are saints. Merciless competition is in evidence. There are men, and women too, with hard, fierce faces and with hard, pitiless hearts who think no more of murdering a person in order to gain their ends than most of us do of killing a mosquito that annoys us. The gentle, trusting soul often enough has his trust and confidence abused and frequently discovers that unscrupulous people take advantage of the " easy mark ". There are ages of " struggle for existence " behind us and " the fittest to survive " have often been the strongest and the best " fighters ". If " the way of the transgressor is hard ", it would also seem to be true that the way of the soft and gentle optimist is no less difficult to maintain.

I do not blink any of these facts, and the list of hard realities could run on to much greater length and still be true. This is certainly not " the best possible world "—I can think of a much better one—and if the word " optimist " is to be taken in its superlative sense I am not one of that extreme type. What I am contending for as a working principle is the faith that the world *can be* remoulded nearer to our hearts' desire, that we can rebuild the moral and spiritual world, and

that we can do it by the cultivation of a new spirit,
by the practice of a new way of life and by loyalty
to ideals of love, co-operation and fellowship. The
important question, as Phillips Brooks used to say, is
whether, in our admittedly checker-board world of
black and white, the black squares are on a white
background, or the white squares on a black background. It is a deep-seated Quaker faith that the
permanent background is white, not black, and that
the ultimate nature of the universe backs the aims that
are true and the things that are good.

This method of faith in the remoulding of the world
will meet with defeats as well as with victories. Christ
was allowed only three years of ministry, love and
service before He was hurried to the cross and His
way of life condemned by the prevailing " interests " of
the day. " Away with this man ! " they cried. " Give
us Barabbas ; we can understand *his* methods." Yes,
but that cross did not terminate Christ's way of life.
It proved to be one of its greatest energies and springs
of power. It laid a spell on men's hearts. It won
the soul of a thief and bandit who was dying within
sight of it. It powerfully moved the centurion who
beheld it. It conquered the young scholar from Tarsus
and it became his battle-cry, " I will not glory in anything save the Cross of Christ." It brought the greatest
Carthaginian that ever lived, Augustine of Hippo, to
this way of life. It was the inspiration and power in
the life of that poor little man of Assisi, as it is to-day
in the life and work of Gandhi. There has been no
other conqueror to be compared with the Galilean.
" Art thou a king ? " Pilate asked, and the bold answer
came, " To this end was I born and for this cause
came I into the world that I might bear witness to the

truth." He has been ruling and conquering ever since Pilate yielded and pronounced his sentence. Who knows whether *defeat* may not sometimes be more important than so-called victories ? Are " lost causes " really *lost* ? In any case, we need not be disturbed by the fact that the world is organized on a basis of strength, force and power, and that the " new way " can win only by slow stages and through defeats and pain and suffering. All we need to know at present is that the new way is the right way and that the universe is so constructed that in the end this new way can prevail.

A few years ago a girl was lost in the streets of London and disappeared. The woman who was her guardian finally traced her to one of the darkest dives in one of the worst sections of the city. Alone and unguarded the lady went to the house and knocked. A man with a terrible face answered the knock. She was swept with a sense of fear as she saw him, but she reached in her pocket, drew out a well-filled purse, handed it to the man and asked him if he would keep it safely for her while she went on an errand into the house. He took it, the lady went in, searched the place, found the girl and returned to the door. As they were about to go out, the thug-like man stepped forward, handed her the purse and, with tears in his eyes said, " That is the first time in my life any one has ever trusted me." A medical missionary whom I know and love went two years ago on an expedition, with a few companions, in a small motor-boat to investigate an island to see if it would do for a leper colony, where these unfortunates could have remedial treatment. On the return trip the boat was boarded by a band of dangerous bandits, who infested a near-by island. The doctor calmly told the leader of the gang about their plans for the relief of the lepers for whom they had come and said to him, " We knew that you were here, but we came just the same and we brought no arms to defend ourselves." The bandit was deeply touched and withdrew with his men without having harmed any person or having taken a thing from the boat. The softening of hard hearts does not perhaps always follow the experiment of trust and confidence, but it very often does follow and it may be said that the method works as well as any human method does.

The Quakers have never assumed that the new world was to be built by miracle or that it would be a light and easy matter to swing over from the way of force to the way of love. They have suffered and agonized through many wars in which they could not take part. They have endured the despoiling of goods, the hostile cry of hate and sometimes even the loss of life, because they would not share in the old way of force and carnage. Their position has often appeared absurd. They seem to ignore facts. It looks as though they were living in a fool's paradise and nursing an insane dream. " Would you let a thug kill your wife, burn your house, carry off your goods, and do nothing to restrain him ? " The problem of how to deal with the thug—and incidentally, as I have shown, the Quakers have dealt with that problem on many occasions very successfully—offers no real parallel to the methods of war. Nations are not thugs. They are bodies of intelligent people. Their claims and causes and charges are either just or unjust. They would practically never push their claims, causes and charges to extreme issue if they were met with kindness, intelligence and wisdom by the nation with whom they are in dispute.

In any case, fighting will not settle whether the claims were just or unjust. It will only settle which nation can mobilize and handle its fighting forces and its economic forces the better. When the war ends, it will be found that there was an equal amount of " thuggery " practised on both sides, that terrible things were done to force the final victory. Multitudes of innocent persons will have suffered. The little children of the two countries will be the main victims. Lands will be made desolate. Social progress will be arrested. The poor will be swamped with taxes for an entire generation. The mutilated men will drag out a broken life to the end of their days. A large part of the " facts " used to arouse patriotism and to stir the fervour and the fierceness of the fighting spirit will be discovered to have been " propaganda ". And yet not one single thing will have been done to determine where right or justice or truth lay in the issues involved.

In view of these things, Friends are pledged to another way of life. They will not ally themselves to the way of war, nor to its methods or its deeds. It is difficult, of course, to live in a world *which is being made.* We build our cities on strata of the earth which may without a moment's warning break, slip, tilt, quake and shake the entire city down into a heap of ruins. These catastrophes used to be attributed to God ; we now see that it is a human risk which we ourselves take when we construct a city on a strip of the earth's crust which is only partly finished. Still less finished is man himself, and least of all the social fabric upon which we must build our systems and our ideals. We are still in the infancy of the race. The diseases of childhood are not all over. The moods and passions of unripe years occasionally sweep in and disturb the household. It is bound to be difficult trying to live by ideals for which the slowly maturing world is not quite ready. But it is the price that must be paid for prophetic vision and it is a risk well worth taking.

The alternative would be to refuse to follow any vision of life which ran ahead of the settled practice of society, to decline to deviate from the customs and habits of one's time and to wait for the better conditions of life until they " emerge " from the sky, or peradventure " come " by the sheer drive of evolution, or until by some happy chance the race all together decides to " leap " to a new height. The alternative is a vain hope. Social progress is not inevitable. It is not like the escalator, the moving staircase, which goes steadily on and carries the climber upward whether he walks or not. There is an inherent risk attaching to our social partnerships. We cannot be persons without being woven into a social group, and, alas, the group to which we belong is not on an escalator. If it goes upwards, it will be because some of us who belong to it take the risk of practising a forward-looking vision ; because we are ready to make hard sacrifices for a truth that has broken in on our souls ; because we are done with the old pettifogging methods in vogue and take the chances and the penalties of trying an advance.

But these visions of advance must not be just pious aspirations, subjects for drawing-room conversation when we have exhausted the possibilities of the weather, nor must they be mere propaganda-topics for lecture halls and " forums ". Visions of advance are things to be done, not to be easily talked about. They are ways of living, not dreams of a sleeper. The Quakers have been primarily *doers*. They believe strongly in the laboratory method. They try their experiment and then proceed to interpret it. The words, the talk, come after the deeds. The psychologists tell us now that *we are built for action*, though the hosts of theorists belie that view. It is Quaker faith that war can be eliminated only by a way of life that first eliminates hate, greed, fear, jealousy, rivalry, injustice, misunderstanding, misjudging and overreaching. But so long as that faith is only an untested theory, it is nothing but a pious hope. The Quaker has endeavoured to try it, to make an experiment with it, in the interwoven tissues of social life. Having started his experiment in peace times, he cannot give it up and resort to the methods of hate and fear as soon as war is declared. He believes that it is a matter of a good deal of importance to have a body of people, even though it may be a small body, who will not surrender their ideal—their vision of advance—even in the face of the earthquake and the broken strata. It is worth something to have the lighted torch held high, when others have allowed the swirl of the storm to blow theirs out.

The only way the new kind of world will eventually come will be through the persistence, the patience and the unyielding faith of those who will not surrender, nor compromise, nor mistake expediency for truth. We must have our Thermopylæs of peace and our spiritual Bunker Hills, where a little band of heroic persons are ready to stand the opposing world and to show that in the end the right way becomes the way men live.

It is, of course, much more than a question of war and peace between nations. The method which I am presenting—the new spirit—applies to all the affairs of life. We cannot very well get our " new world " of international relations until we find out how to eliminate the catastrophes of war. We must somehow make our house secure against these periodic earthquakes, but it is no less important to reorganize, on the same principle, our business operations, our family life, our political systems, and our ecclesiastical fellowships. Hates and fears and rivalries are not confined to the international sphere. The wastes which our present civilization entails are not limited to periods of war. We waste the precious raw material of the earth all the time. Our haste and rivalry, our fear that somebody will get ahead of us in exploiting the rich deposits in the soil of the earth are squandering the limited stock of supplies, which ought to be handled with the utmost care and conserved for those who will come after us. But much more serious is the waste of human life. We exploit men and women and children as well as coal and oil. We build our cities for the ease and convenience of commerce, not for the promotion of life and happiness. The slum is an outrage against humanity. The narrow, treeless streets, without gardens and breathing spaces for the play of the children, are marks of selfishness, ignorance and stupidity. The mills and factories and mines, where labour is massed, where initiative and creative qualities are eliminated, where a person is largely reduced to a mechanistic tool, involve a large sum total both of blunders and sins against palpitating human beings whom God has made.

We are all part of it and we are all responsible for the evil conditions, and we shall never have a " new world " here until we wake up and want it and are ready to pay the high price which it will cost. There is once more no escalator for this. It will come only as we make experiments with another way of living. The process of advance begins with a vision of advance. The little heroic band—like those men in the pass at Thermopylæ and Warren's men at Bunker Hill—must make the stand, fling out their banner and dare the venture. It means once more the practice of a new spirit rather than the abstract formulation of a new theory of society. It means the brave adoption of a new way of living. It involves greater simplicity of life, more sacrifices, more love and sympathy, less selfishness and rivalry. It cannot be claimed, I am sorry to say, that the Quakers have held to this ideal with the same consistency with which they have laboured for peace. But they have had a few leaders who have held up a clear torch and who have had the courage to obey their heavenly vision. Success and prosperity have come to many Friends. They have acquired goods and standing and they have profited by the ways and methods now in vogue. Nevertheless there are many of them, often including those who are well supplied with the things of the world, who are dedicated to the business of producing the new spirit and creating the new world. Most Friends are at least " tender " in these matters. They do not know how to go to work to build the better world, they are not sure what advance step to take first, how to rebuild the house while we are still living in it, but they do have sensitive hearts, awakened minds and brave spirits to dare the forward step when they see it.

" When they see it " is a very important condition in this business of building the world. Sentiment, enthusiasm, desire, consecration are not enough. None of us would want for our sick child a doctor who had only those qualities. When the doctor arrives he must know what ails the child and he must furthermore know how to get him out of his fever into health. We want the consecration and the desire, but we want none the less skill and knowledge. The task of prescribing for a human society sick with many ailments is surely not easier than the curing of the disordered child. It is strange that we should suppose that while the child needs skill, the social order, on the other hand, needs only enthusiasm and eagerness. Unless we are prepared for worse ills than we already have, we must not lose our heads, shut our eyes and submit our blind jugdments to empiric guides with a quick panacea, who expect to conjure forth social health by " projecting " an arm-chair theory. These guides admit that the first effect of their treatment may be worse than the present state. They say " things must be worse before they are better ". They comfort us with the phrase, " You cannot get an omelet without breaking eggs ". But the deeper question is whether the breaking of the eggs will really insure the omelet. There are grave chances that even the best possible shift of social and economic schemes will not cure our patient and that after the eggs are smashed we shall get only burnt omelet.

The trouble lies deeper. Our real problem is the formation of the right spirit. No changes in the proportions of wealth and poverty would be adequate, though they might produce favouring conditions. No political reorganizations would work the miracle. Sooner or later we must learn to love and trust one another. We must form the habit of sharing and co-operating. We must be as ready to sacrifice as we now are to compete. There is no substitute for the new spirit and the new way of life. We shall need experts, wise guides, persons who have clear insight and sound wisdom, but with experts or no experts, we shall never get our happy, joyous, peaceful world until we learn to love and understand and share and become brothers to one another, because we are children of a common Father.

The cultivation and practice of this spirit are essential features of Quakerism. The building of the new world is its programme. I cannot claim that there are impressive " exhibits " to which I can point. I cannot assert that the achievements of these two hundred and fifty years are startling. There has been a good deal of blundering in those years, and wasted energy. There have been periods of quietism. There have been aspirations for the making of a " peculiar people ". There have been Quakers who have wanted a strict, exclusive sect, withdrawn from the world. There have been among them stern, narrow theologians who were absorbed in the minutiæ of doctrine. There have been controversies and separations over points of difference that had nothing to do with this new spirit or the new world or with the building of the kingdom of God. The onward line of march has been again and again interrupted by will-o'-the-wisps and wandering fires. There have been unnecessary wilderness-wanderings and retrograde curves. But in spite of all this, the body has been slowly going forward. It has never altogether forgotten its divine mission. It has vitally held to its practice of spiritual worship and to its faith in human progress. It has always had, even in its darker periods, some leaders of vision and of wisdom who have maintained the onward *direction*.

They have called it back from its speculations and theories to its experimental basis. They have revived the visions of advance and have renewed the experiment of love and faith. They have raised their voices for the quiet, patient way of the Spirit. They have believed in the truth of the ancient proverb: " God empties the nest by hatching out the eggs ", which means that instead of smashing the eggs, God lets the life within slowly push forth in power and potency and change the old situation by processes of birth and development. In the main, Quaker faith has taken this line and has lived in this hope.

INDEX

179